The Two Gentlemen of Verona

In Plain and Simple English

BookCaps™ Study Guides

www.bookcaps.com

© 2012. All Rights Reserved.

Table of Contents

ABOUT THIS SERIES 3

CHARACTERS 4

PLAY 6

    ACT I 7
        SCENE I. Verona. *8*
        SCENE II. The same. *18*
        SCENE III. The same. *29*
    ACT II..34
        SCENE I. Milan. *35*
        SCENE II. Verona. *47*
        SCENE III. The same. *49*
        SCENE IV. Milan. *53*
        SCENE V. The same. *68*
        SCENE VI. The same. *72*
        SCENE VII. Verona. *75*
    ACT III 80
        SCENE I. Milan. *81*
        SCENE II. The same. *105*
    ACT IV 111
        SCENE I. The frontiers of Mantua. *112*
        SCENE II. Milan. *118*
        SCENE III. The same. *128*
        SCENE IV. The same. *131*
    ACT V 143
        SCENE I. Milan. *144*
        SCENE II. The same. *145*
        SCENE III. The frontiers of Mantua. *150*
        SCENE IV. Another part of the forest. *152*

About This Series

The "Classic Retold" series started as a way of telling classics for the modern reader—being careful to preserve the themes and integrity of the original. Whether you want to understand Shakespeare a little more or are trying to get a better grasps of the Greek classics, there is a book waiting for you!

The series is expanding every month. Visit BookCaps.com to see all the books in the series, and while you are there join the Facebook page, so you are first to know when a new book comes out.

Characters

DUKE OF MILAN, father to Silvia

VALENTINE, one of the two gentlemen

PROTEUS, one of the two gentlemen

ANTONIO, father to Proteus

THURIO, a foolish rival to Valentine

EGLAMOUR, agent for Silvia in her escape

SPEED, a clownish servant to Valentine

LAUNCE, the like to Proteus

PANTHINO, servant to Antonio

HOST, where Julia lodges in Milan

OUTLAWS, with Valentine

JULIA, a lady of Verona, beloved of Proteus

SILVIA, beloved of Valentine

LUCETTA, waiting-woman to Julia

SERVANTS

MUSICIANS

Play

ACT I

SCENE I. Verona.

An open place.

Enter VALENTINE and PROTEUS

VALENTINE
Cease to persuade, my loving Proteus:
Stop trying to convince me, my dear Proteus:
Home-keeping youth have ever homely wits.
Young people who stay at home have very dull minds.
Were't not affection chains thy tender days
If passion didn't chain your youthful days
To the sweet glances of thy honour'd love,
To the sweet glances of the woman you love,
I rather would entreat thy company
I would ask for your company
To see the wonders of the world abroad,
To see the wonders of the world abroad,
Than, living dully sluggardized at home,
Instead of you living lazily and idly at home,
Wear out thy youth with shapeless idleness.
And wearing out your youth with aimless spare time.
But since thou lovest, love still and thrive therein,
But since you are in love, continue to love and let your love flourish,
Even as I would when I to love begin.
Just as I would when I fall in love.

PROTEUS
Wilt thou be gone? Sweet Valentine, adieu!
Are you leaving? Sweet Valentine, farewell!
Think on thy Proteus, when thou haply seest
Think of your friend Proteus, who you see by chance
Some rare note-worthy object in thy travel:
Something rare and note-worthy in your travels:
Wish me partaker in thy happiness
Wish that I could join in on your happiness
When thou dost meet good hap; and in thy danger,
When you meet with good fortune; and in your danger,
If ever danger do environ thee,

If ever danger surrounds you,
Commend thy grievance to my holy prayers,
Entrust your suffering to my holy prayers,
For I will be thy beadsman, Valentine.
For I will pray for you, Valentine.

VALENTINE
And on a love-book pray for my success?
And will you pray on a book of love that I will succeed?

PROTEUS
Upon some book I love I'll pray for thee.
I'll pray for you on some book that I love.

VALENTINE
That's on some shallow story of deep love:
That would be the silly story of true love:
How young Leander cross'd the Hellespont.
Of young Leander who swam across the Hellespont, which connects the Aegean and Marmara Seas.

PROTEUS
That's a deep story of a deeper love:
That's a deep story of a truer love:
For he was more than over shoes in love.
For he was more than shoe deep in love.

VALENTINE
'Tis true; for you are over boots in love,
It's true; for you more than boot deep in love,
And yet you never swum the Hellespont.
And you still have never swum across the Hellespont.

PROTEUS
Over the boots? nay, give me not the boots.
More than boot deep? No, don't make fun of me.

VALENTINE
No, I will not, for it boots thee not.
No, I won't, because it won't help you.

PROTEUS
What?
What?

VALENTINE

To be in love, where scorn is bought with groans;
To be in love is to be where whimpers lead to ridicule;
Coy looks with heart-sore sighs; one fading moment's mirth
Heart-sick sighs are given disdainful looks; where one brief moment of happiness
With twenty watchful, weary, tedious nights:
Is paired with twenty wide-awake, sleepless and tedious nights:
If haply won, perhaps a hapless gain;
If by chance your love is won, perhaps it is an unfortunate achievement;
If lost, why then a grievous labour won;
And if it is lost, then he has only achieved a sorrowful struggle;
However, but a folly bought with wit,
Whatever happens, it's only a mistake gained with wisdom,
Or else a wit by folly vanquished.
Or else wisdom destroyed by a mistake.

PROTEUS

So, by your circumstance, you call me fool.
So, by your descriptions, you think that I'm a fool.

VALENTINE

So, by your circumstance, I fear you'll prove.
So, in your situation, I'm afraid you will prove yourself to be one.

PROTEUS

'Tis love you cavil at: I am not Love.
It's love itself that you dispute with: I am not Love.

VALENTINE

Love is your master, for he masters you:
Love is your master, because he control you:
And he that is so yoked by a fool,
And man that is controlled by a fool,
Methinks, should not be chronicled for wise.
I think, should not be labeled as being wise.

PROTEUS

Yet writers say, as in the sweetest bud
But writers say that just as in the sweetest flower
The eating canker dwells, so eating love
Lives a destructive worm, so does destructive love
Inhabits in the finest wits of all.
Live in the finest minds of all.

VALENTINE

And writers say, as the most forward bud
And writers say that just as the earliest flower
Is eaten by the canker ere it blow,
Is destroyed by the worm before it blossoms,
Even so by love the young and tender wit
So does love turn the young and tender mind
Is turn'd to folly, blasting in the bud,
Into a fool, withering in the bud,
Losing his verdure even in the prime
Losing his vitality just at his prime
And all the fair effects of future hopes.
And all the excellent outcomes that the future might bring.
But wherefore waste I time to counsel thee,
But why do I waste my time giving you advice,
That art a votary to fond desire?
You who are a worshipper of foolish desire?
Once more adieu! my father at the road
Once more, farewell! At the harbor, my father
Expects my coming, there to see me shipp'd.
Is waiting for my arrival, to see me off to sea.

PROTEUS

And thither will I bring thee, Valentine.
And I will bring you there, Valentine.

VALENTINE

Sweet Proteus, no; now let us take our leave.
Sweet Proteus, no; let us say our goodbyes now.
To Milan let me hear from thee by letters
While I'm in Milan, send me letters to tell me
Of thy success in love, and what news else
Of your fortune in love, and what other news
Betideth here in absence of thy friend;
Takes place here in the absence of your friend;
And likewise will visit thee with mine.
And I will send you letters with news of my endeavors.

PROTEUS

All happiness bechance to thee in Milan!
May you only have happiness happen to you in Milan!

VALENTINE

As much to you at home! and so, farewell.
And the same to you at home! And now, good bye.

Exit

PROTEUS
He after honour hunts, I after love:
He hunts after honor, and I hunt after love:
He leaves his friends to dignify them more,
He leaves his friends to bring more honor to them,
I leave myself, my friends and all, for love.
And I leave myself, my friends and everyone, for love.
Thou, Julia, thou hast metamorphosed me,
You, Julia, you have transformed me,
Made me neglect my studies, lose my time,
Made me neglect my studies, waste my time,
War with good counsel, set the world at nought;
Argue with good advice, and consider the world worthless;
Made wit with musing weak, heart sick with thought.
It's made my mind weak from pondering, and my heart sick from worry.

Enter SPEED

SPEED
Sir Proteus, save you! Saw you my master?
Sir Proteus, God save you! Have you seen my master?

PROTEUS
But now he parted hence, to embark for Milan.
Just now he left here to set off for Milan.

SPEED
Twenty to one then he is shipp'd already,
Twenty to one odds that he has boarded the ship already then,
And I have play'd the sheep in losing him.
And I have made a big mistake in losing him.

PROTEUS
Indeed, a sheep doth very often stray,
It's true, a sheep might very often wander off,
An if the shepherd be a while away.
If the shepherd isn't near.

SPEED

You conclude that my master is a shepherd, then,
Are you saying that my master is a shepherd, then,
and I a sheep?
And I am a sheep?

PROTEUS
I do.
I am.

SPEED
Why then, my horns are his horns, whether I wake or sleep.
Well then, since he is my master, my horns are his horns, whether I am awake or asleep.

PROTEUS
A silly answer and fitting well a sheep.
That's a silly answer and one that fits a sheep well.

SPEED
This proves me still a sheep.
This still shows me to be a sheep.

PROTEUS
True; and thy master a shepherd.
True; and your master is a shepherd.

SPEED
Nay, that I can deny by a circumstance.
No, that I can refute with a good explanation.

PROTEUS
It shall go hard but I'll prove it by another.
It will go badly, but I'll prove it to be so by another explanation.

SPEED
The shepherd seeks the sheep, and not the sheep the
The shepherd seeks the sheep, and the sheep doesn't seek the
shepherd; but I seek my master, and my master seeks
Shepherd; but I seek my master, and my master doesn't seek
not me: therefore I am no sheep.
Me: therefore I am not a sheep.

PROTEUS
The sheep for fodder follow the shepherd; the

The sheep follows the shepherd for food; the
shepherd for food follows not the sheep: thou for
Shepherd doesn't follow the sheep for food: you
wages followest thy master; thy master for wages
Follow your master for your pay; the master
follows not thee: therefore thou art a sheep.
Doesn't follow you for pay: therefore you are a sheep.

SPEED

Such another proof will make me cry 'baa.'
Another explanation like that one will make me 'baa' like a sheep.

PROTEUS

But, dost thou hear? gavest thou my letter to Julia?
But are you listening? Did you give my letter to Julia?

SPEED

Ay sir: I, a lost mutton, gave your letter to her,
Yes sir: I, just a lost sheep, gave your letter to her,
a laced mutton; and she, a laced mutton, gave me, a
A lacy whore; and she, a lacy whore, gave me, a
lost mutton, nothing for my labour.
Lost sheep, nothing for my efforts.

PROTEUS

Here's too small a pasture for such store of muttons.
This place is too small of a pasture for so many sheep.

SPEED

If the ground be overcharged, you were best stick her.
If the land is overstocked, it you be better for you to kill her.

PROTEUS

Nay: in that you are astray, 'twere best pound you.
No: in that you are wrong, it would be best for me to put you in the pound.

SPEED

Nay, sir, less than a pound shall serve me for
No, sir, less than a pound will pay me for
carrying your letter.
Carrying your letter.

PROTEUS

You mistake; I mean the pound,--a pinfold.

You are mistaken; I mean the pound—the pen for stray animals.

SPEED
From a pound to a pin? fold it over and over,
Down from a pound to a penny? Multiply that over and over,
'Tis threefold too little for carrying a letter to   ·
It's three-times too little for carrying a letter to
your lover.
You lover.

PROTEUS
But what said she?
But what did she say?

SPEED
[First nodding] Ay.
[He nods first and then speaks] Yes, she nodded, 'aye'.

PROTEUS
Nod--Ay--why, that's noddy.
Nod—'Aye'—well, that's 'noddy', a fool.

SPEED
You mistook, sir; I say, she did nod: and you ask
You misunderstood, sir; I said that she nodded: and you asked
me if she did nod; and I say, 'Ay.'
Me if she nodded; and I say, 'Aye.'

PROTEUS
And that set together is noddy.
And when you put that together it's 'noddy', which means a fool.

SPEED
Now you have taken the pains to set it together,
You are the one who has troubled yourself to put it together,
take it for your pains.
Take the name as a reward for your trouble.

PROTEUS
No, no; you shall have it for bearing the letter.
No, no; it's your reward for carrying the letter.

SPEED
Well, I perceive I must be fain to bear with you.

Well, I guess I must carry the name with you.

PROTEUS
Why sir, how do you bear with me?
Well sir, how do you carry with me?

SPEED
Marry, sir, the letter, very orderly; having nothing
By Mary, sir, the letter I carried very properly; being given nothing
but the word 'noddy' for my pains.
But the word 'noddy' for my trouble.

PROTEUS
Beshrew me, but you have a quick wit.
Devil take me, you have a very quick mind.

SPEED
And yet it cannot overtake your slow purse.
But still my quick mind isn't a match for your slow money-pouch.

PROTEUS
Come come, open the matter in brief: what said she?
Come on, relate the subject-matter quickly: what did she say?

SPEED
Open your purse, that the money and the matter may
Open your purse so that the money and the subject-matter may
be both at once delivered.
Be given at the same time.

"[PROTEUS gives SPEED a coin]"

PROTEUS
Well, sir, here is for your pains. What said she?
Well, sir, here is payment for your troubles. What did she say?

SPEED
Truly, sir, I think you'll hardly win her.
To tell the truth, sir, I don't think you'll win her over.

PROTEUS
Why, couldst thou perceive so much from her?
Why, could you tell that much from her?

SPEED
Sir, I could perceive nothing at all from her; no,
Sir, I could get nothing from her at all; no,
not so much as a ducat for delivering your letter:
Not even a gold coin for delivering your letter:
and being so hard to me that brought your mind, I
And since she was so hard on me, who brought the letter expressing your feelings, I'm
fear she'll prove as hard to you in telling your
Afraid she'll end up being just as hard on you when you tell her your
mind. Give her no token but stones; for she's as
Feelings in person. Don't give her any tokens of your affection except for jewels; for she's as
hard as steel.
Hard as steel.

PROTEUS
What said she? nothing?
What did she say? Nothing?

SPEED
No, not so much as 'Take this for thy pains.' To
No, not even, 'Take this for your troubles.' To
testify your bounty, I thank you, you have testerned
Respond to your gift, I thank you, you have tipped me a six-pence;
me; in requital whereof, henceforth carry your
In repayment of that, after this you can carry your
letters yourself: and so, sir, I'll commend you to my master.
Letters yourself: and so, sir, I'll give your greetings to my master.

PROTEUS
Go, go, be gone, to save your ship from wreck,
Go, go on, go away, go save your ship from wrecking,
Which cannot perish having thee aboard,
Because it cannot wreck if you are aboard,
Being destined to a drier death on shore.
Since you are destined to a death by hanging on the shore.

Exit SPEED

I must go send some better messenger:
I must go send some better messenger:
I fear my Julia would not deign my lines,
I'm afraid that my Julia wouldn't accept my words,
Receiving them from such a worthless post.
Since she was receiving them from such a worthless messenger.

Exit

SCENE II. The same.

Garden of JULIA's house.

Enter JULIA and LUCETTA

JULIA
But say, Lucetta, now we are alone,
Tell me, Lucetta, now that we are alone,
Wouldst thou then counsel me to fall in love?
Would you advise me to fall in love?

LUCETTA
Ay, madam, so you stumble not unheedfully.
Yes, madam, providing that you don't fall carelessly.

JULIA
Of all the fair resort of gentlemen
Of all the splendid crowd of gentlemen
That every day with parle encounter me,
That meets me with conversation everyday,
In thy opinion which is worthiest love?
In your opinion which is the worthiest of my love?

LUCETTA
Please you repeat their names, I'll show my mind
Please, repeat their names for me, I'll tell you what I think
According to my shallow simple skill.
Based on my silly simple observations.

JULIA
What think'st thou of the fair Sir Eglamour?
What do you think of the excellent Sir Eglamour?

LUCETTA
As of a knight well-spoken, neat and fine;
As a knight he is well-spoken, elegant and refined;
But, were I you, he never should be mine.
But, if I were you, he would never be my lover.

JULIA

What think'st thou of the rich Mercatio?
What do you think of the rich Mercatio?

LUCETTA
Well of his wealth; but of himself, so so.
I think well of his wealth; but of him as a person, he's so-so.

JULIA
What think'st thou of the gentle Proteus?
What do you think of the noble Proteus?

LUCETTA
Lord, Lord! to see what folly reigns in us!
Dear Lord! To see how silly we women can be!

JULIA
How now! what means this passion at his name?
What's this! Why this passionate outburst when name him?

LUCETTA
Pardon, dear madam: 'tis a passing shame
Forgive me, dear madam: it's a supreme shame
That I, unworthy body as I am,
That I, unworthy servant that I am,
Should censure thus on lovely gentlemen.
Should pass judgment like this on a loving gentlemen.

JULIA
Why not on Proteus, as of all the rest?
Why should you not pass judgment on Proteus as you did for the rest of them?

LUCETTA
Then thus: of many good I think him best.
I will say this: of the many good men, I think he is the best.

JULIA
Your reason?
What's your reason?

LUCETTA
I have no other, but a woman's reason;
I have no reason but a woman's reason;
I think him so because I think him so.
I think he's the best because I think he's the best.

JULIA
And wouldst thou have me cast my love on him?
And would you have me give him my love?

LUCETTA
Ay, if you thought your love not cast away.
Yes, if you thought your love was not being wasted.

JULIA
Why he, of all the rest, hath never moved me.
Why, out of all of them, he has never made a move on me.

LUCETTA
Yet he, of all the rest, I think, best loves ye.
But out of all of them, I think he loves you the most.

JULIA
His little speaking shows his love but small.
His few words about it show that his love is not that much.

LUCETTA
Fire that's closest kept burns most of all.
Passion that's kept closest to the chest burns most of all.

JULIA
They do not love that do not show their love.
They are not in love if they don't show their love.

LUCETTA
O, they love least that let men know their love.
Oh, the ones who let everyone know of their love, love the least.

JULIA
I would I knew his mind.
I wish I knew what he was thinking.

LUCETTA
Peruse this paper, madam.
Read this letter, madam.

JULIA
'To Julia.' Say, from whom?
'To Julia.' Tell me, who is this from?

LUCETTA
That the contents will show.
The contents of the letter will tell you that.

JULIA
Say, say, who gave it thee?
Tell me, tell me, who gave it to you?

LUCETTA
Valentine's page; and sent, I think, from Proteus.
Valentine's servant; and I think it was sent from Proteus.
He would have given it you; but I, being in the way,
He would have given it to you; but since I met him first, I
Did in your name receive it: pardon the
Received it for you: forgive me the
fault I pray.
Mistake, please.

JULIA
Now, by my modesty, a goodly broker!
Now, as I swear by my own modesty, a good go-between!
Dare you presume to harbour wanton lines?
Do you dare to hide passionate letters from me?
To whisper and conspire against my youth?
To whisper behind my back and plot against my youth?
Now, trust me, 'tis an office of great worth
Now, believe me, it's a role of great importance
And you an officer fit for the place.
and you are someone fit for that role.
Or else return no more into my sight.
If not, don't let me see you again.

LUCETTA
To plead for love deserves more fee than hate.
To ask for love deserves higher payment than hate does.

JULIA
Will ye be gone?
Will you leave?

LUCETTA
That you may ruminate.
I will so that you may think.

Exit

JULIA
And yet I would I had o'erlooked the letter:
And still I wish I had read the letter:
It were a shame to call her back again
It would be a shame to call her back again
And pray her to a fault for which I chid her.
And ask her to make a mistake that I scolded her for.
What a fool is she, that knows I am a maid,
What a fool she is, who know I am a virgin,
And would not force the letter to my view!
And would not make me read the letter!
Since maids, in modesty, say 'no' to that
Since virgins, in their modesty, say 'no' to whatever
Which they would have the profferer construe 'ay.'
They want the giver to interpret as 'yes.'
Fie, fie, how wayward is this foolish love
Shame, for shame, how awkward is this foolish love
That, like a testy babe, will scratch the nurse
That, like an irritable baby, will scratch her nurse
And presently all humbled kiss the rod!
And immediately afterward become meek and obedient!
How churlishly I chid Lucetta hence,
How harshly I drove away Lucetta just now,
When willingly I would have had her here!
When I would gladly have her be here!
How angerly I taught my brow to frown,
How angrily I scowled my face,
When inward joy enforced my heart to smile!
When inwardly joy made my heart smile!
My penance is to call Lucetta back
My punishment for this is to call Lucetta back
And ask remission for my folly past.
And ask forgiveness for my mistake just then.
What ho! Lucetta!
Come here! Lucetta!

Re-enter LUCETTA

LUCETTA
What would your ladyship?
What do you need, my lady?

JULIA
Is't near dinner-time?
Is it near dinner time?

LUCETTA
I would it were,
I wish it were,
That you might kill your stomach on your meat
So that you might satisfy your anger with your meal
And not upon your maid.
Instead taking it out on your servant.

"[JULIA bends over and picks up the letter.]"

JULIA
What is't that you took up so gingerly?
What did you just pick up so carefully?

LUCETTA
Nothing.
Nothing.

JULIA
Why didst thou stoop, then?
Why did you bend over, then?

LUCETTA
To take a paper up that I let fall.
To pick up the paper that I dropped.

JULIA
And is that paper nothing?
And is that paper nothing?

LUCETTA
Nothing concerning me.
It's nothing that is of importance to me.

JULIA
Then let it lie for those that it concerns.
Then let it stay where it is for those who it is of importance to.

LUCETTA
Madam, it will not lie where it concerns
Madam, it will not tell lies about its content
Unless it have a false interpeter.
Unless it has a dishonest reader.

JULIA
Some love of yours hath writ to you in rhyme.
Some lover of yours has written you a poem.

LUCETTA
That I might sing it, madam, to a tune.
So that I might sing it as a song, madam.
Give me a note: your ladyship can set.
Give me a melody: you can compose the song, my lady.

JULIA
As little by such toys as may be possible.
I put as little effort into such games as I can.
Best sing it to the tune of 'Light o' love.'
You'd better sing it to the tune of 'Light of Love.'

LUCETTA
It is too heavy for so light a tune.
It is to serious for such a lighthearted tune.

JULIA
Heavy! belike it hath some burden then?
Serious! Perhaps it has a chorus then?

LUCETTA
Ay, and melodious were it, would you sing it.
Yes, and if it has a melody, you would sing it.

JULIA
And why not you?
Why would I sing it and not you?

LUCETTA
I cannot reach so high.
I can't sing that high.

JULIA
Let's see your song. How now, minion!

Let's hear your song. Come on, hussy!

LUCETTA
Keep tune there still, so you will sing it out:
You have the same temper and tune, if you keep it up you'll finish the song and lose your mood:
And yet methinks I do not like this tune.
And still I don't think that I like this song.

JULIA
You do not?
You don't?

LUCETTA
No, madam; it is too sharp.
No, madam; it is too high-pitched.

JULIA
You, minion, are too saucy.
You, hussy, are too insolent.

LUCETTA
Nay, now you are too flat
No, now you are too low-pitched
And mar the concord with too harsh a descant:
And mess up the harmony with too an accompaniment that is too harsh:
There wanteth but a mean to fill your song.
Your song lacks a middle-part to fill it out.

JULIA
The mean is drown'd with your unruly bass.
The middle-part is drowned out by your rowdy low-voice.

LUCETTA
Indeed, I bid the base for Proteus.
Yes, I'm singing on behalf of Proteus.

JULIA
This babble shall not henceforth trouble me.
This nonsense will not bother me anymore.
Here is a coil with protestation!
Here is the proof of my displeasure!

Tears the letter

Go get you gone, and let the papers lie:
Go, get away from here, and let the papers stay where they are:
You would be fingering them, to anger me.
you would pick them up just to anger me.

LUCETTA
She makes it strange; but she would be best pleased
She pretends to not care; but she would be very happy
To be so anger'd with another letter.
to have another letter make her so angry.

Exit

JULIA
Nay, would I were so anger'd with the same!
No, I wish I were still angry with the same letter!
O hateful hands, to tear such loving words!
Oh, my terrible hand that tore apart those loving words!
Injurious wasps, to feed on such sweet honey
Harmful wasps that feed on such sweet honey
And kill the bees that yield it with your stings!
And kill the bees that make it by stinging them!
I'll kiss each several paper for amends.
I'll kiss each and every paper to make amends.
Look, here is writ 'kind Julia.' Unkind Julia!
Look, here it says 'kind Julia.' Cruel Julia!
As in revenge of thy ingratitude,
In revenge of your ungratefulness, Julia
I throw thy name against the bruising stones,
I'll throw the name Julia against hurtful stones,
Trampling contemptuously on thy disdain.
And scornfully trample on your contempt.
And here is writ 'love-wounded Proteus.'
And here is written, 'love-sick Proteus.'
Poor wounded name! my bosom as a bed
Poor love-sick man! My breast pocket will hold the letter and my hear will hold you
Shall lodge thee till thy wound be thoroughly heal'd;
Until your love is completely healed.
And thus I search it with a sovereign kiss.
And so I'll clean your wound with a healing kiss.
But twice or thrice was 'Proteus' written down.
Only two are three times was Proteus' name written down.
Be calm, good wind, blow not a word away

May the breeze stay calm so it doesn't blow a word away
Till I have found each letter in the letter,
Until I have found every piece of the letter,
Except mine own name: that some whirlwind bear
Except where my own name is written: that some breeze can carry
Unto a ragged fearful-hanging rock
Off a jagged and frightening overhanging rock
And throw it thence into the raging sea!
and throw it from there into the raging sea!
Lo, here in one line is his name twice writ,
Look, here on one line his name it written twice,
'Poor forlorn Proteus, passionate Proteus,
'Poor desperate Proteus, passionate Proteus,
To the sweet Julia:' that I'll tear away.
To the sweet Julia:' that part I'll tear away.
And yet I will not, sith so prettily
And still I won't tear it since so prettily
He couples it to his complaining names.
He pairs my name with his pitiful names.
Thus will I fold them one on another:
So I will fold them together:
Now kiss, embrace, contend, do what you will.
Now kiss, hold close, sexually embrace, do whatever you want.

Re-enter LUCETTA

LUCETTA
Madam,
Madam,
Dinner is ready, and your father stays.
Dinner is ready, and your father is waiting.

JULIA
Well, let us go.
Well, let's go then.

LUCETTA
What, shall these papers lie like tell-tales here?
What, and leave these papers to lie here like little signs?

JULIA
If you respect them, best to take them up.
If you value them then you'd better clean them up?

LUCETTA
Nay, I was taken up for laying them down:
No, I was scolded for picking them up:
Yet here they shall not lie, for catching cold.
But there will not stay here in case the wind blows them away.

JULIA
I see you have a month's mind to them.
I see you have a fondness for them.

LUCETTA
Ay, madam, you may say what sights you see;
Yes, madam, you may say what you think;
I see things too, although you judge I wink.
I see things too, and while you judge what you see, I close my eyes to it.

JULIA
Come, come; will't please you go?
Come on; would you like to go?

Exeunt

SCENE III. The same.

ANTONIO's house.

Enter ANTONIO and PANTHINO

ANTONIO
Tell me, Panthino, what sad talk was that
Panthino, tell me, what was the serious talk with
Wherewith my brother held you in the cloister?
Which my brother kept you in courtyard?

PANTHINO
'Twas of his nephew Proteus, your son.
It was about his nephew Proteus, your son.

ANTONIO
Why, what of him?
Why, what about him?

PANTHINO
He wonder'd that your lordship
He was discussing how your lordship
Would suffer him to spend his youth at home,
Allows him to spend the days of his youth at home,
While other men, of slender reputation,
While other men of lesser standing,
Put forth their sons to seek preferment out:
Send their sons off to seek social advancement:
Some to the wars, to try their fortune there;
Some go to war to try their luck there;
Some to discover islands far away;
Some go to discover islands far away;
Some to the studious universities.
Some go to the academic universities.
For any or for all these exercises,
For any and all of these activities,
He said that Proteus your son was meet,
He said that your son Proteus was suitable,
And did request me to importune you

And he asked me to urge you
To let him spend his time no more at home,
To not let him spend his time at home any more,
Which would be great impeachment to his age,
Which would be a great disservice to him when he is older,
In having known no travel in his youth.
To not have travelled in his youth.

ANTONIO
Nor need'st thou much importune me to that
You don't need to urge me to do that
Whereon this month I have been hammering.
Since during this month I have been thinking hard.
I have consider'd well his loss of time
I have certainly considered the loss of his youthful days
And how he cannot be a perfect man,
And how he can't be an accomplished man,
Not being tried and tutor'd in the world:
If he has not been put to the test and learned from being out in the world:
Experience is by industry achieved
Experience is earned by hard work
And perfected by the swift course of time.
And perfected in time as it flies by.
Then tell me, whither were I best to send him?
Tell me then, where should I send him?

PANTHINO
I think your lordship is not ignorant
I believe your lordship is not unaware
How his companion, youthful Valentine,
That his friend, the young Valentine,
Attends the emperor in his royal court.
Is at the royal court of the emperor.

ANTONIO
I know it well.
I know that well.

PANTHINO
'Twere good, I think, your lordship sent him thither:
It would be good, I think, if your lordship send him there:
There shall he practise tilts and tournaments,
There he can practice jousting and tournaments,
Hear sweet discourse, converse with noblemen.

Hear fine conversation, associate himself with noblemen.
And be in eye of every exercise
And be able to see every custom
Worthy his youth and nobleness of birth.
That is appropriate of his youth and noble birth.

ANTONIO
I like thy counsel; well hast thou advised:
I like your advice: you have advised me well:
And that thou mayst perceive how well I like it,
And so that you may see how well I like it,
The execution of it shall make known.
I will carry it out to show you.
Even with the speediest expedition
With the quickest haste
I will dispatch him to the emperor's court.
I will send him away to the emperor's court.

PANTHINO
To-morrow, may it please you, Don Alphonso,
Tomorrow, if you like, Don Alphonso,
With other gentlemen of good esteem,
And other gentlemen of high status,
Are journeying to salute the emperor
Are travelling to pay their respects to the emperor
And to commend their service to his will.
And to hand over their service to his command.

ANTONIO
Good company; with them shall Proteus go:
They are good company; Proteus will go with them:
And, in good time! now will we break with him.
And soon! No we will tell him about this.

Enter PROTEUS

PROTEUS
Sweet love! sweet lines! sweet life!
Sweet love! Sweet words! Sweet life!
Here is her hand, the agent of her heart;
Here is her handwriting, which conveys her feelings;
Here is her oath for love, her honour's pawn.
Here is her promise of love, her pledge of honor.
O, that our fathers would applaud our loves,

32

Oh, how our fathers will approve of our love,
To seal our happiness with their consents!
And finalize our happiness with their consent to our marriage!
O heavenly Julia!
Oh, heavenly Julia!

ANTONIO
How now! what letter are you reading there?
What's this! What letter are you reading there?

PROTEUS
May't please your lordship, 'tis a word or two
If you would like to know, my lord, it's a letter
Of commendations sent from Valentine,
Of good wishes sent from Valentine,
Deliver'd by a friend that came from him.
Delivered to me by a friend that he sent.

ANTONIO
Lend me the letter; let me see what news.
Hand me the letter; let me see what news it tells.

PROTEUS
There is no news, my lord, but that he writes
There is no news, my lord, he just writes on
How happily he lives, how well beloved
How happily he's living, how he's well liked
And daily graced by the emperor;
And daily favored by the emperor;
Wishing me with him, partner of his fortune.
And wishes that I were with him, as partner to his good fortune.

ANTONIO
And how stand you affected to his wish?
And how do you feel about his wish?

PROTEUS
As one relying on your lordship's will
I feel that it relies on what you want, my lord,
And not depending on his friendly wish.
And doesn't depend on my friend's wish.

ANTONIO
My will is something sorted with his wish.

What I want is somewhat in agreement with his wish.
Muse not that I thus suddenly proceed;
Don't be surprised that I so suddenly bring this up;
For what I will, I will, and there an end.
Since what I want, I want and there the discussion ends.
I am resolved that thou shalt spend some time
I am determined that you will spend some time
With Valentinus in the emperor's court:
With Valentine in the emperor's court:
What maintenance he from his friends receives,
What funds he received from his friends,
Like exhibition thou shalt have from me.
As an allowance you will receive from me.
To-morrow be in readiness to go:
Tomorrow be ready to go:
Excuse it not, for I am peremptory.
Don't decline, because I am absolutely decided.

PROTEUS
My lord, I cannot be so soon provided:
My lord, I can't be ready so soon:
Please you, deliberate a day or two.
Please, think about to for a day or two.

ANTONIO
Look what thou want'st shall be sent after thee:
Whatever you need will be gathered for you:
No more of stay! to-morrow thou must go.
Don't talk anymore of staying! Tomorrow you will go.
Come on, Panthino: you shall be employ'd
Come on, Panthino: you will work
To hasten on his expedition.
To make his journey come together quickly.

Exeunt ANTONIO and PANTHINO

PROTEUS
Thus have I shunn'd the fire for fear of burning,
And so I have jumped away from the fire since I was afraid to be burned
And drench'd me in the sea, where I am drown'd.
And soaked myself in the sea instead, where I have drowned
I fear'd to show my father Julia's letter,
I was afraid to show Julia's letter to my father,
Lest he should take exceptions to my love;

34

In case he should disprove of my love;
And with the vantage of mine own excuse
And with the use of my own excuse
Hath he excepted most against my love.
He has made the biggest obstacle to my love.
O, how this spring of love resembleth
Oh, how this love is like spring, and resembles
The uncertain glory of an April day,
The uncertain beauty of a day in April,
Which now shows all the beauty of the sun,
Which in one moment is sunny and beautiful,
And by and by a cloud takes all away!
And in another a cloud takes all that away!

Re-enter PANTHINO

PANTHINO
Sir Proteus, your father calls for you:
Sir Proteus, your father is asking for you:
He is in haste; therefore, I pray you to go.
He is in a hurry: so, I ask you to please go.

PROTEUS
Why, this it is: my heart accords thereto,
Well, this is it: my heart agrees to this,
And yet a thousand times it answers 'no.'
But still it says 'no' a thousand times and is reluctant to leave.

Exeunt

ACT II

SCENE I. Milan.

The DUKE's palace.

Enter VALENTINE and SPEED

SPEED
Sir, your glove.
Sir, here's your glove.

VALENTINE
Not mine; my gloves are on.
It's not mine; my gloves are on.

SPEED
Why, then, this may be yours, for this is but one.
Well, then, take it anyway, since it's only one of a pair.

VALENTINE
Ha! let me see: ay, give it me, it's mine:
Ha! Let me see it: yes, give it to me, it's mine:
Sweet ornament that decks a thing divine!
What a sweet article of clothing that was worn by such a lovely woman!
Ah, Silvia, Silvia!
Ah, Silvia, Silvia!

SPEED
Madam Silvia! Madam Silvia!
Madam Silvia! Madam Silvia

VALENTINE
How now, sirrah?
What are you doing, man?

SPEED
She is not within hearing, sir.
She's not within hearing distance, sir.

VALENTINE
Why, sir, who bade you call her?
Tell me, sir, who asked you to call for her?

SPEED
Your worship, sir; or else I mistook.
You did, my lord; or else I misunderstood.

VALENTINE
Well, you'll still be too forward.
Well, you're always too hasty.

SPEED
And yet I was last chidden for being too slow.
But last time I was scolded for being too slow.

VALENTINE
Go to, sir: tell me, do you know Madam Silvia?
Get on with it, sir: tell me, do you know Madam Silvia?

SPEED
She that your worship loves?
The woman that you love, my lord?

VALENTINE
Why, how know you that I am in love?
Well, how do you know that I am in love?

SPEED
Marry, by these special marks: first, you have
By Mary, by these certains signs: first off, you have
learned, like Sir Proteus, to wreathe your arms,
Learned, like Sir Proteus, to cross your arms,
like a malecontent; to relish a love-song, like a
Like someone unhappy; learned to sing a love-song, like the
robin-redbreast; to walk alone, like one that had
Red-breasted songbird; to walk alone, like one who is
the pestilence; to sigh, like a school-boy that had
Ill; to sigh, like a schoolboy who has
lost his A B C; to weep, like a young wench that had
Lost his school books; to weep, like a young girl who has
buried her grandam; to fast, like one that takes
Just buried her grandmother; to not eat, like someone who's on a
diet; to watch like one that fears robbing; to
Diet; to stay awake at night, like someone who's afraid to be robbed; to
speak puling, like a beggar at Hallowmas. You were

Speak with a whimper, like a beggar on All Saint's Day. You used to be
wont, when you laughed, to crow like a cock; when you
Accustomed to crow like a cock, when you laughed; when you
walked, to walk like one of the lions; when you
Walked, you did so like a lion; when you
fasted, it was presently after dinner; when you
Didn't eat, it was right after dinner; when you
looked sadly, it was for want of money: and now you
Looked upset, it was because you needed money: and now you
are metamorphosed with a mistress, that, when I look
Have been transformed by a lady, so that, when I look
on you, I can hardly think you my master.
At you, I can hardly recognize my master.

VALENTINE
Are all these things perceived in me?
You can see all of these things in my presence?

SPEED
They are all perceived without ye.
I can see all of them out of your presence.

VALENTINE
Without me? they cannot.
When I'm not around? You can't.

SPEED
Without you? nay, that's certain, for, without you
When you're not around? No, that's for sure, since—unless you
were so simple, none else would: but you are so
Were so simple—no one would; but you are so
without these follies, that these follies are within
Opposed to these silly things, that when you're doing these silly things
you and shine through you like the water in an
They are as obvious as water is in an
urinal, that not an eye that sees you but is a
Urinal, so that not a single person sees you who isn't a
physician to comment on your malady.
Doctor to comment on your sickness.

VALENTINE
But tell me, dost thou know my lady Silvia?
But tell me, do you know my lady Silvia?

SPEED
She that you gaze on so as she sits at supper?
The woman that you stare at like that while she sits at supper?

VALENTINE
Hast thou observed that? even she, I mean.
Have you noticed that? I mean, her.

SPEED
Why, sir, I know her not.
Well, sir, I don't know her.

VALENTINE
Dost thou know her by my gazing on her, and yet
Do you only know her from me staring at her, but
knowest her not?
Not know her?

SPEED
Is she not hard-favoured, sir?
Isn't she unattractive, sir?

VALENTINE
Not so fair, boy, as well-favoured.
At just pretty, boy, but very attractive.

SPEED
Sir, I know that well enough.
Sir, I know that well enough.

VALENTINE
What dost thou know?
What do you know?

SPEED
That she is not so fair as, of you, well-favoured.
That she is not just pretty but very attractive to you.

VALENTINE
I mean that her beauty is exquisite, but her favour infinite.
I mean that her beauty is exquisite, but her attractiveness is endless.

SPEED
That's because the one is painted and the other out

That's because one of them is artificial on and the other is
of all count.
Beyond measureing.

VALENTINE
How painted? and how out of count?
How is it artificial? And how beyond measure?

SPEED
Marry, sir, so painted, to make her fair, that no
By Mary, sir, so painted with make-up to make her pretty, that no
man counts of her beauty.
Man values her beauty.

VALENTINE
How esteemest thou me? I account of her beauty.
What do you think of me? I value her beauty.

SPEED
You never saw her since she was deformed.
You haven't seen her since she was disfigured.

VALENTINE
How long hath she been deformed?
How long has she been disfigured?

SPEED
Ever since you loved her.
Ever since you began to love her.

VALENTINE
I have loved her ever since I saw her; and still I
I have loved her ever since I saw her; and still I
see her beautiful.
Think she is beautiful.

SPEED
If you love her, you cannot see her.
If you love her, you cannot see her.

VALENTINE
Why?
Why not?

SPEED
Because Love is blind. O, that you had mine eyes;
Because Love is blind. Oh, if only you could see through my eyes;
or your own eyes had the lights they were wont to
Or if your own eyes saw how they used to
have when you chid at Sir Proteus for going
When you would nag at Sir Proteus for going
ungartered!
Without his garters as a love-sick man does!

VALENTINE
What should I see then?
What would I see then?

SPEED
Your own present folly and her passing deformity:
Your own current foolishness and her extreme deformity:
for he, being in love, could not see to garter his
For Proteus, when he was in love, could not see to but on his
hose, and you, being in love, cannot see to put on your hose.
Garters, and you, now that you are in love, cannot see to put on your pants.

VALENTINE
Belike, boy, then, you are in love; for last
Perhaps, boy, then, you are in love; for yesterday
morning you could not see to wipe my shoes.
Morning you couldn't see to clean my shoes.

SPEED
True, sir; I was in love with my bed: I thank you,
It's true, sir; I was in love with my bed: I'll tell you,
you swinged me for my love, which makes me the
You beat me for my love, which makes me all the more
bolder to chide you for yours.
Brave to scold you for yours.

VALENTINE
In conclusion, I stand affected to her.
In conclusion, I stand totally in love with her.

SPEED
I would you were set, so your affection would cease.
I wish you were calmly seated, so your love would end.

VALENTINE
Last night she enjoined me to write some lines to
Last night she urged me to write a letter to
one she loves.
Someone she loves.

SPEED
And have you?
And have you?

VALENTINE
I have.
I have.

SPEED
Are they not lamely writ?
Are they badly written?

VALENTINE
No, boy, but as well as I can do them. Peace!
No, boy, but written as well as I can. Be calm!
here she comes.
Here she comes.

SPEED
[Aside] O excellent motion! O exceeding puppet!
[Aside] Oh, what a great puppet-show! Oh, what a good puppet she is!
Now will he interpret to her.
Now he will be the puppet-master for her puppet!

Enter SILVIA

VALENTINE
Madam and mistress, a thousand good-morrows.
Madam and mistress, I wish you a thousand good mornings.

SPEED
[Aside] O, give ye good even! here's a million of manners.
[Aside] Oh, not even a good evening! Here's an excessive use of manners.

SILVIA
Sir Valentine and servant, to you two thousand.
Sir Valentine and his servant, may you have two thousand good mornings.

SPEED
[Aside] He should give her interest and she gives it him.
[Aside] He should show his interest in her, and she'll give it back to him double.

VALENTINE
As you enjoin'd me, I have writ your letter
As you asked me, I have written your letter
Unto the secret nameless friend of yours;
To this secret nameless lover of yours;
Which I was much unwilling to proceed in
Which I was very unwilling to do
But for my duty to your ladyship.
Except that it was my duty to you, my lady.

SILVIA
I thank you gentle servant: 'tis very clerkly done.
Thank you, kind follower: it's very cleverly done.

VALENTINE
Now trust me, madam, it came hardly off;
Now believe me, madam, it was hard to do;
For being ignorant to whom it goes
Since I didn't know who it was meant for
I writ at random, very doubtfully.
I wrote randomly, and with uncertainty.

SILVIA
Perchance you think too much of so much pains?
Perhaps you think it was too much trouble?

VALENTINE
No, madam; so it stead you, I will write
No, madam; if it will help you, I will write
Please you command, a thousand times as much; And yet—
If you ask me to, I would do so I thousand times; But still—

SILVIA
A pretty period! Well, I guess the sequel;
A nice little pause! Well, I will guess what was going to come next;
And yet I will not name it; and yet I care not;
But I won't say what it was; and still I don't care;
And yet take this again; and yet I thank you,
But take this back; and thank you,
Meaning henceforth to trouble you no more.

This means after this I won't bother you again.

SPEED
[Aside] And yet you will; and yet another 'yet.'
[Aside] But you will; and still there's another 'but.'

VALENTINE
What means your ladyship? do you not like it?
What do you mean, my lady? Do you not like it?

SILVIA
Yes, yes; the lines are very quaintly writ;
Yes, yes; the letter is very skillfully written;
But since unwillingly, take them again.
But since it was written unwillingly, take it back again.
Nay, take them.
No, take it.

VALENTINE
Madam, they are for you.
Madam, it is for you.

SILVIA
Ay, ay: you writ them, sir, at my request;
Yes, yes: since you wrote it, sir, at my request;
But I will none of them; they are for you;
But I won't take it; you take it;
I would have had them writ more movingly.
I wish you had written it more sincerely.

VALENTINE
Please you, I'll write your ladyship another.
If you want, I'll write another letter for you, my lady.

SILVIA
And when it's writ, for my sake read it over,
And when you've written it, for my sake read over it,
And if it please you, so; if not, why, so.
And if you like it, so be it; and if not, well, so be it.

VALENTINE
If it please me, madam, what then?
If I like it, madam, what do you want me to do then?

SILVIA
Why, if it please you, take it for your labour:
Well, if you like it, take it as payment for you work;
And so, good morrow, servant.
And with that, good morning, my follower.

Exit

SPEED
O jest unseen, inscrutable, invisible,
Oh, what a joke it is that is unseen, mysterious, and invisible
As a nose on a man's face, or a weathercock on a steeple!
Just like a nose is on a man's face, or a weathervane is on a steep roof!
My master sues to her, and she hath
My master pursues her, and she has
taught her suitor,
Taught her admirer,
He being her pupil, to become her tutor.
Since he is her student, to become her teacher.
O excellent device! was there ever heard a better,
Oh what an excellent scheme! Has a better one ever been heard of,
That my master, being scribe, to himself should write
That my master, being a writer, should write to himself
the letter?
The letter?

VALENTINE
How now, sir? what are you reasoning with yourself?
What's this, sir? What are you talking to yourself about?

SPEED
Nay, I was rhyming: 'tis you that have the reason.
No, I was just muttering; it's you who has the good sense.

VALENTINE
To do what?
To do what?

SPEED
To be a spokesman for Madam Silvia.
To speak on the behalf of Madam Silvia.

VALENTINE
To whom?

But who am I speaking to?

SPEED
To yourself: why, she wooes you by a figure.
To yourself: why, she courts you with a scheme.

VALENTINE
What figure?
What scheme?

SPEED
By a letter, I should say.
With a letter, I should have said.

VALENTINE
Why, she hath not writ to me?
But she hasn't written to me?

SPEED
What need she, when she hath made you write to
What should she need to, when she has made you write a letter to
yourself? Why, do you not perceive the jest?
Yourself? What, do you not get the joke?

VALENTINE
No, believe me.
No, I don't, believe me.

SPEED
No believing you, indeed, sir. But did you perceive
There's no believing you, indeed, sir. But did you notice
her earnest?
Her repayment?

VALENTINE
She gave me none, except an angry word.
She gave me nothing but angry words.

SPEED
Why, she hath given you a letter.
Why, she has given you a letter.

VALENTINE
That's the letter I writ to her friend.

That's the letter that I wrote to her lover.

SPEED
And that letter hath she delivered, and there an end.
And she has delivered that letter to that friend, and that's the end of it.

VALENTINE
I would it were no worse.
I wish that were so.

SPEED
I'll warrant you, 'tis as well:
I promise you, it's just that:
For often have you writ to her, and she, in modesty,
For you have often written to her, and she, in her modesty,
Or else for want of idle time, could not again reply;
Or else not having free time, could not sent a reply;
Or fearing else some messenger that might her mind discover,
Or else being afraid that a messenger might find out her feelings,
Herself hath taught her love himself to write unto her lover.
She has taught the man she loves to write to on her behalf to her lover, which is he.
All this I speak in print, for in print I found it.
Everything I say is very specific, since I found it specifically.
Why muse you, sir? 'tis dinner-time.
What are you wondering about, sir? It's dinner time.

VALENTINE
I have dined.
I have already eaten.

SPEED
Ay, but hearken, sir; though the chameleon Love can
Yes, but listen, sir; although Love itself is said to change its shape
feed on the air, I am one that am nourished by my
And feed on air, I am a man that is fed by my
victuals, and would fain have meat. O, be not like
Food, and would gladly have some meat. Oh, don't be like
your mistress; be moved, be moved.
Your mistress; be persuaded, sympathize.

Exeunt

SCENE II. Verona.

JULIA'S house.

Enter PROTEUS and JULIA

PROTEUS
Have patience, gentle Julia.
Be patient, kind Julia.

JULIA
I must, where is no remedy.
I must be, there is nothing else I can do.

PROTEUS
When possibly I can, I will return.
Whenever I can, I will return.

JULIA
If you turn not, you will return the sooner.
If you don't change your mind about me, you will return all the sooner because of it.
Keep this remembrance for thy Julia's sake.
Keep this love-token to remember your Julia.

Giving a ring
"[JULIA give PROTEUS a ring]"

PROTEUS
Why then, we'll make exchange; here, take you this.
Whell then, we'll exchange love-tokens; here, take this.

"[PROTEUS gives JULIA a ring]"

JULIA
And seal the bargain with a holy kiss.
And we'll seal the exchange with a holy kiss

PROTEUS
Here is my hand for my true constancy;
Here is my promise for my honest loyalty;
And when that hour o'erslips me in the day

And if an hour passes unnoticed in a day
Wherein I sigh not, Julia, for thy sake,
Where I don't sigh, for you Julia,
The next ensuing hour some foul mischance
May the hours after that contain some dreadful misfortune
Torment me for my love's forgetfulness!
To punish me for forgetting my love!
My father stays my coming; answer not;
My father is waiting for me to arrive; don't answer;
The tide is now: nay, not thy tide of tears;
The time has come: no, not the time of tears;
That tide will stay me longer than I should.
For your tears will not keep me longer than I can stay.
Julia, farewell!
Julia, goodbye!

Exit JULIA

What, gone without a word?
What, she leaves without a word?
Ay, so true love should do: it cannot speak;
Yes, that's how true love should be: it cannot speak;
For truth hath better deeds than words to grace it.
For the truth is shown in actions, not in words.

Enter PANTHINO

PANTHINO
Sir Proteus, you are stay'd for.
Sir Proteus, they are waiting for you.

PROTEUS
Go; I come, I come.
Go on; I'm coming, I'm coming.
Alas! this parting strikes poor lovers dumb.
Sadly, this departure makes us unfortunate lovers speechless.

Exeunt

SCENE III. The same.

A street.

Enter LAUNCE, leading a dog

LAUNCE
Nay, 'twill be this hour ere I have done weeping;
Now, I will have finished crying before this hour is over:
all the kind of the Launces have this very fault. I
My whole family of Launces suffer from this same weakness. I
have received my proportion, like the prodigious
Have received my payment, like the son who leaves and returns again,
son, and am going with Sir Proteus to the Imperial's
And I am going with Sir Protues to the emperor's
court. I think Crab, my dog, be the sourest-natured
Court. I think my dog, Crab, is the most grumpy-natured
dog that lives: my mother weeping, my father
Dog that lives: my mother was weeping, my father
wailing, my sister crying, our maid howling, our cat
Sobbing, my sister crying, our maid howling, our cat was
wringing her hands, and all our house in a great
Holding her paws in grief, and our whole house was in a great
perplexity, yet did not this cruel-hearted cur shed
Confusion, but this cruel-hearted mutt didn't shed a
one tear: he is a stone, a very pebble stone, and
Single tear: he is made of stone, a very worthless stone, and
has no more pity in him than a dog: a Jew would have
Is as pitiless as a dog: even a pitiless Jew would have
wept to have seen our parting; why, my grandam,
Wept if he had seen our goodbyes: why, my grandmother,
having no eyes, look you, wept herself blind at my
Who has no eyes, you understand, wept until she was blind
parting. Nay, I'll show you the manner of it. This
When I left. No, I'll demonstrate how it happened. This
shoe is my father: no, this left shoe is my father:
Shoe represents my father: no, this left shoe is I my father:
no, no, this left shoe is my mother: nay, that
No, no, this left shoes is my mother instead: no, it
cannot be so neither: yes, it is so, it is so, it

Can't be either of them: yes, it's like this, it's like this, it
hath the worser sole. This shoe, with the hole in
Has a worse sole than the other. This shoe, with the hole in
it, is my mother, and this my father; a vengeance
It, is my mother, and this other one is my father; curse
on't! there 'tis: now, sit, this staff is my
It! There it is: now, stay like that, this cane is my
sister, for, look you, she is as white as a lily and
Sister, since, look at this, she is as white as a lily and
as small as a wand: this hat is Nan, our maid: I
As slender as a pole: this hat is our maid, Nan: I
am the dog: no, the dog is himself, and I am the
Represent the dog: no, the dog represents me, Launce, and I am the
dog--Oh! the dog is me, and I am myself; ay, so,
Dog—Oh! The dog represents me, and I am myself; yes, that's how it is,
so. Now come I to my father; Father, your blessing:
That's how it is. Now I'm getting to talking about my father; First, I asked him for permission:
now should not the shoe speak a word for weeping:
Then, the shoe that is my father couldn't say a word because he was crying:
now should I kiss my father; well, he weeps on. Now
Then I kissed my father goodbye; he continued to cry. Then
come I to my mother: O, that she could speak now
I went to my mother: Oh, if only she could speak now
like a wood woman! Well, I kiss her; why, there
Like a mad woman! Well, I kissed her; well, there
'tis; here's my mother's breath up and down. Now
It is; that's how my mother smells exactly. Then
come I to my sister; mark the moan she makes. Now
I went to my sister; notice how she was wailing. Then
the dog all this while sheds not a tear nor speaks a
That whole time this dog didn't shed a tear or say a
word; but see how I lay the dust with my tears.
Word; but notice how I'm laying in the dirt with my tears.

Enter PANTHINO

PANTHINO
Launce, away, away, aboard! thy master is shipped
Launce, come on, come one, get on board! Your master is on the ship
and thou art to post after with oars. What's the
And you are to quickly follow after him. What's the
matter? why weepest thou, man? Away, ass! You'll
Matter? Why are you crying, man? Come on, you ass! You'll
lose the tide, if you tarry any longer.

lose the sea current if you wait any more.

LAUNCE
It is no matter if the tied were lost; for it is the
It's be no big deal if the dog were lost; for he is the
unkindest tied that ever any man tied.
Meanest dog that any man ever tied up.

PANTHINO
What's the unkindest tide?
What's the meanest dog?

LAUNCE
Why, he that's tied here, Crab, my dog.
Well, this one here, Crab, my dog.

PANTHINO
Tut, man, I mean thou'lt lose the flood, and, in
Shame on you, man, I mean you'll lose the current and by
losing the flood, lose thy voyage, and, in losing
Losing the current, you'll miss the trip, and by missing
thy voyage, lose thy master, and, in losing thy
The trip, you'll lose your master, and but losing your
master, lose thy service, and, in losing thy
Master, lose your job, and by losing your
service,--Why dost thou stop my mouth?
Job—why are you shushing me?

LAUNCE
For fear thou shouldst lose thy tongue.
Because I'm afraid you'll lose your tongue.

PANTHINO
Where should I lose my tongue?
Why would I lose my tongue?

LAUNCE
In thy tale.
From telling that story.

PANTHINO
In thy tail!
It's your ass on the line!

LAUNCE
Lose the tide, and the voyage, and the master, and
Lose the current, and the trip, and the master, and
the service, and the tied! Why, man, if the river
The job, and the dog! Well, man, if the river
were dry, I am able to fill it with my tears; if the
Were dry, I would be able to fill it with my tears; if the
wind were down, I could drive the boat with my sighs.
Winds were gone, I could sail the boat with my sighs.

PANTHINO
Come, come away, man; I was sent to call thee.
Come on, come on, man; I was sent here to bring you.

LAUNCE
Sir, call me what thou darest.
Sir, call me whatever your dare to

PANTHINO
Wilt thou go?
Will you go?

LAUNCE
Well, I will go.
Well, I'll go.

Exeunt

SCENE IV. Milan.

The DUKE's palace.

Enter SILVIA, VALENTINE, THURIO, and SPEED

SILVIA
Servant!
Followers!

VALENTINE
Mistress?
Mistress?

SPEED
Master, Sir Thurio frowns on you.
Mister, Sir Thurio is not happy with you.

VALENTINE
Ay, boy, it's for love.
Yes, boy, it's because of my love.

SPEED
Not of you.
Not your love.

VALENTINE
Of my mistress, then.
The love of my mistress, then.

SPEED
'Twere good you knocked him.
It would be good if you beat him.

Exit

SILVIA
Servant, you are sad.
My follower, you are sad.

VALENTINE

Indeed, madam, I seem so.
Yes, madam, I seem to be sad.

THURIO
Seem you that you are not?
Do you think you are not sad?

VALENTINE
Haply I do.
Perhaps I am.

THURIO
So do counterfeits.
So are liars.

VALENTINE
So do you.
So are you.

THURIO
What seem I that I am not?
What did I do to seem that way?

VALENTINE
Wise.
You're wise

THURIO
What instance of the contrary?
What proof is there against that?

VALENTINE
Your folly.
Your mistakes.

THURIO
And how quote you my folly?
And what mistake did you notice?

VALENTINE
I quote it in your jerkin.
I notice it in your jacket.

THURIO

My jerkin is a doublet.
My jacket is a coat.

VALENTINE
Well, then, I'll double your folly.
Well, then, that's twice the mistake.

THURIO
How?
How so?

SILVIA
What, angry, Sir Thurio! do you change colour?
What, are you angry, Sir Thurio! Do you change moods like that?

VALENTINE
Give him leave, madam; he is a kind of chameleon.
Let him go, madam; he changes moods like a chameleon changes color.

THURIO
That hath more mind to feed on your blood than live
You had better make sure that you take care of your body rather than live
in your air.
In your head.

VALENTINE
You have said, sir.
You speak the truth, sir.

THURIO
Ay, sir, and done too, for this time.
Yes, sir, and done with that too, for now.

VALENTINE
I know it well, sir; you always end ere you begin.
I know how you do that, sir; you always end before you begin.

SILVIA
A fine volley of words, gentlemen, and quickly shot off.
A fine combat of words, gentlemen, and quickly fired.

VALENTINE
'Tis indeed, madam; we thank the giver.
It was indeed, madam; we thank the one who gave us that battle.

SILVIA
Who is that, servant?
Who would that be, my follower?

VALENTINE
Yourself, sweet lady; for you gave the fire. Sir
You, sweet lady; for you gave us the reason to. Sir
Thurio borrows his wit from your ladyship's looks,
Thurio borrows his intelligence from your looks, my lady,
and spends what he borrows kindly in your company.
And spends his borrowed intelligence lovingly when you're around.

THURIO
Sir, if you spend word for word with me, I shall
Sir, if you trade words with me, I will
make your wit bankrupt.
Empty out your intelligence.

VALENTINE
I know it well, sir; you have an exchequer of words,
I know that, sir; you have a bank account filled with words,
and, I think, no other treasure to give your
And, I think, no other currency to give to your
followers, for it appears by their bare liveries,
Servants, since by the look of their shabby uniforms,
that they live by your bare words.
They are paid with only your words.

SILVIA
No more, gentlemen, no more:--here comes my father.
Stop it, gentlemen, stop it—here comes my father.

Enter DUKE

DUKE
Now, daughter Silvia, you are hard beset.
Now, my daughter Silvia, you are sincerely surrounded by men.
Sir Valentine, your father's in good health:
Sir Valentine, your father is in good health:
What say you to a letter from your friends
What would you say to a letter from you friends
Of much good news?
With a lot of good news?

VALENTINE
My lord, I will be thankful.
My lord, I would be thankful
To any happy messenger from thence.
Of any messenger with good news from them.

DUKE
Know ye Don Antonio, your countryman?
Do you know, Don Antonio, a man from your same homeland?

VALENTINE
Ay, my good lord, I know the gentleman
Yes, my good lord, I know that gentlemen
To be of worth and worthy estimation
To be of wealth and high esteem
And not without desert so well reputed.
And he's not so well respected without cause.

DUKE
Hath he not a son?
Does he have a son?

VALENTINE
Ay, my good lord; a son that well deserves
Yes, my good lord; a son that also deserves
The honour and regard of such a father.
The honor and affection of a father like Don Antonio.

DUKE
You know him well?
Do you know him well?

VALENTINE
I know him as myself; for from our infancy
I know him as well as I know myself; because since we were babies
We have conversed and spent our hours together:
We have been friends and spent our days together:
And though myself have been an idle truant,
And though I have been an lazy shirker,
Omitting the sweet benefit of time
Forgetting about the sweet benefit that time provides
To clothe mine age with angel-like perfection,

To supply my old age with angel-like perfection,
Yet hath Sir Proteus, for that's his name,
Sir Proteus, for that's his name, has instead
Made use and fair advantage of his days;
Made improvements and good use of his time;
His years but young, but his experience old;
He is still young, but he has the experience of someone older;
His head unmellow'd, but his judgment ripe;
His head shows no grey hairs, but his judgment is mature;
And, in a word, for far behind his worth
And, in short, for his worth is far beyond
Comes all the praises that I now bestow,
All the praises I am giving him now,
He is complete in feature and in mind
He is accomplished in looks and in mind
With all good grace to grace a gentleman.
With all the good grace that a gentleman should have.

DUKE
Beshrew me, sir, but if he make this good,
Curse me, sir, but if he is this good
He is as worthy for an empress' love
He is worthy of the love of an empress
As meet to be an emperor's counsellor.
And suitable to me an emperor's advisor.
Well, sir, this gentleman is come to me,
Well, sir, this gentleman has come to me
With commendation from great potentates;
With recommendations from very powerful rules;
And here he means to spend his time awhile:
And he means to spend some time here for a while:
I think 'tis no unwelcome news to you.
I think this is welcome news to you.

VALENTINE
Should I have wish'd a thing, it had been he.
If I had wished for such a thing, it would be for him to come.

DUKE
Welcome him then according to his worth.
Then welcome him according to his importance.
Silvia, I speak to you, and you, Sir Thurio;
Silvia, I am talking to you, and you, Sir Thurio, when I say that;
For Valentine, I need not cite him to it:

Because I don't need to urge Valentine to do that:
I will send him hither to you presently.
I will send him to you here shortly.

Exit

VALENTINE
This is the gentleman I told your ladyship
This is the gentleman that I told your lady ship about who
Had come along with me, but that his mistress
Would have come along with me, except that his mistress
Did hold his eyes lock'd in her crystal looks.
Kept him there chained to her beauty.

SILVIA
Belike that now she hath enfranchised them
Perhaps now she has freed him
Upon some other pawn for fealty.
For some other oath of loyalty.

VALENTINE
Nay, sure, I think she holds them prisoners still.
No, I'm sure, I think she hold him prisoner still.

SILVIA
Nay, then he should be blind; and, being blind
No, then he should be blind; and, being blind,
How could he see his way to seek out you?
How could he see his way to find you?

VALENTINE
Why, lady, Love hath twenty pair of eyes.
Why, lady, Love has twenty pairs of eyes.

THURIO
They say that Love hath not an eye at all.
They say that Love is blind.

VALENTINE
To see such lovers, Thurio, as yourself:
Love is when he sees such lovers as yourself, Thurio:
Upon a homely object Love can wink.
He can close his eyes to an ugly man.

SILVIA
Have done, have done; here comes the gentleman.
Stop it, stop it; here comes the gentleman.

Exit THURIO

Enter PROTEUS

VALENTINE
Welcome, dear Proteus! Mistress, I beseech you,
Welcome, dear Proteus! Mistress, I ask you, please
Confirm his welcome with some special favour.
Back up his welcome wit some special honor.

SILVIA
His worth is warrant for his welcome hither,
His worth is permission enough for his welcome here,
If this be he you oft have wish'd to hear from.
If this the man you have often wanted to hear from.

VALENTINE
Mistress, it is: sweet lady, entertain him
Mistress, it is: sweet lady, employ him
To be my fellow-servant to your ladyship.
To be a your follower like me, your lady.

SILVIA
Too low a mistress for so high a servant.
I am to lowly a mistress for such a respected follower.

PROTEUS
Not so, sweet lady: but too mean a servant
That's not true, sweet lady: I am too unworthy a follower
To have a look of such a worthy mistress.
To look upon such a lovely mistress.

VALENTINE
Leave off discourse of disability:
Stop talking of your inadequacies:
Sweet lady, entertain him for your servant.
Sweet lady, take him on as your follower.

PROTEUS
My duty will I boast of; nothing else.

I will brag about my duties as a follower; nothing else.

SILVIA
And duty never yet did want his meed:
And duty has never lacked a rewardL
Servant, you are welcome to a worthless mistress.
My follower, you are welcome to follow an unworthy mistress.

PROTEUS
I'll die on him that says so but yourself.
I'll die fighting whoever that, except for you, yourself.

SILVIA
That you are welcome?
Anyone who says that you're welcome?

PROTEUS
That you are worthless.
Anyone who says that you are worthless.

Re-enter THURIO

THURIO
Madam, my lord your father would speak with you.
Madam, my lord, your father the duke, would like to speak with you.

SILVIA
I wait upon his pleasure. Come, Sir Thurio,
I will grant his wish. Come on, Sir Thurio,
Go with me. Once more, new servant, welcome:
Come with me. Once more, new follower, welcome:
I'll leave you to confer of home affairs;
I'll leave you two to discuss news from home;
When you have done, we look to hear from you.
When you are done, we'd like to hear from you.

PROTEUS
We'll both attend upon your ladyship.
We'll both follow you, your lady.

Exeunt SILVIA and THURIO

VALENTINE
Now, tell me, how do all from whence you came?

Now, tell me, how is everything back home?

PROTEUS
Your friends are well and have them much commended.
Your friends are all doing well and have asked me to send you their greetings.

VALENTINE
And how do yours?
And how are yours?

PROTEUS
I left them all in health.
I left them all doing well.

VALENTINE
How does your lady? and how thrives your love?
How is your lady? And how has your love blossomed?

PROTEUS
My tales of love were wont to weary you;
My tales of love used to annoy you;
I know you joy not in a love discourse.
I know you don't enjoy talking about love.

VALENTINE
Ay, Proteus, but that life is alter'd now:
Yes, Proteus, but life is changed now:
I have done penance for contemning Love,
I have paid the price for despising Love,
Whose high imperious thoughts have punish'd me
Who has punished me with those commanding passions,
With bitter fasts, with penitential groans,
With terrible lack of appetite, with remorseful moaning,
With nightly tears and daily heart-sore sighs;
With tears every night, and heart-aching sighs every day;
For in revenge of my contempt of love,
For in revenge of my contempt of love
Love hath chased sleep from my enthralled eyes
Love has kept my captivated eyes from sleeping
And made them watchers of mine own heart's sorrow.
And made them stay wide-awake to see my own heart ache.
O gentle Proteus, Love's a mighty lord,
Oh, gentle Proteus, Love is a mighty lord,
And hath so humbled me, as, I confess,

And he has brought me so low, that, I admit,
There is no woe to his correction,
There is no punishment worse than that of Love,
Nor to his service no such joy on earth.
Neither is there any other joy on earth that compares to following him.
Now no discourse, except it be of love;
Now, we'll talk of nothing except love;
Now can I break my fast, dine, sup and sleep,
Now I can stop my hunger, and have dinner, supper and sleep,
Upon the very naked name of love.
Talking of the mere name of love.

PROTEUS
Enough; I read your fortune in your eye.
Enough; I could tell what had happened to you from your eyes.
Was this the idol that you worship so?
Who is the woman that you love so much?

VALENTINE
Even she; and is she not a heavenly saint?
The one just here; and isn't she a heavenly angel?

PROTEUS
No; but she is an earthly paragon.
No; she is only a mortal without equals.

VALENTINE
Call her divine.
Call her divine.

PROTEUS
I will not flatter her.
I won't flatter her.

VALENTINE
O, flatter me; for love delights in praises.
Oh, flatter me; since love enjoys compliments.

PROTEUS
When I was sick, you gave me bitter pills,
When I was love-sick, you treated me with harsh comments,
And I must minister the like to you.
And I will give you the same.

VALENTINE
Then speak the truth by her; if not divine,
Then tell the truth about her; if she isn't a goddess,
Yet let her be a principality,
Still she is among the angels,
Sovereign to all the creatures on the earth.
Ruler of all the creatures on the earth.

PROTEUS
Except my mistress.
Except my mistress.

VALENTINE
Sweet, except not any;
Sweet man, there are no exceptions;
Except thou wilt except against my love.
Except the one you take against my love.

PROTEUS
Have I not reason to prefer mine own?
Don't I have a reason to prefer my own love?

VALENTINE
And I will help thee to prefer her too:
And I will help you promote your love too:
She shall be dignified with this high honour—
She will be privileged with this great honor—
To bear my lady's train, lest the base earth
To carry my lady's train, so that the lowly earth
Should from her vesture chance to steal a kiss
Doesn't have the chance to touch her dress
And, of so great a favour growing proud,
And so that, growing proudly from such a great favor,
Disdain to root the summer-swelling flower
Flowers cannot take root in her clothing
And make rough winter everlastingly.
And rough winter will last forever.

PROTEUS
Why, Valentine, what braggardism is this?
Why, Valentine, what I are you bragging about?

VALENTINE
Pardon me, Proteus: all I can is nothing

Forgive me, Proteus: everything I can say means nothing
To her whose worth makes other worthies nothing;
To the woman whose worth makes everything else worth nothing;
She is alone.
She is without equal.

PROTEUS
Then let her alone.
Then leave her alone.

VALENTINE
Not for the world: why, man, she is mine own,
I wouldn't for the world.: why, man, she is mine,
And I as rich in having such a jewel
And I am as rich by having her
As twenty seas, if all their sand were pearl,
As I would be if I had twenty seas with beaches were made of pearls,
The water nectar and the rocks pure gold.
With water made of the drink of the gods, and with rocks of pure gold.
Forgive me that I do not dream on thee,
Forgive me for not paying you too much attention,
Because thou see'st me dote upon my love.
Because you are watching me worshiping my love.
My foolish rival, that her father likes
My foolish rival, who her father likes
Only for his possessions are so huge,
Only because he is rich,
Is gone with her along, and I must after,
Has gone along with her, and I must follow after them,
For love, thou know'st, is full of jealousy.
For love, as you know, is full of jealousy.

PROTEUS
But she loves you?
But does she love you?

VALENTINE
Ay, and we are betroth'd: nay, more, our marriage-hour,
Yes, and we are promised to be married: no, it's rather that, the hour of our marriage,
With all the cunning manner of our flight,
Along with the clever way we will escape,
Determined of; how I must climb her window,
Has been decided; how I will climb to her window on
The ladder made of cords, and all the means

A ladder made of ropes, and all the necessary things
Plotted and 'greed on for my happiness.
For my happiness have been planned for and agreed on.
Good Proteus, go with me to my chamber,
Good Proteus, come with me to my room,
In these affairs to aid me with thy counsel.
And give me your advice on these happenings.

PROTEUS
Go on before; I shall inquire you forth:
Go on ahead of me; I will seek you out:
I must unto the road, to disembark
I must go to the harbor, to send off
Some necessaries that I needs must use,
Some personal necessities that I need,
And then I'll presently attend you.
And then I'll follow you immediately after.

VALENTINE
Will you make haste?
Will you hurry?

PROTEUS
I will.
I will.

Exit VALENTINE

Even as one heat another heat expels,
Just as one fire puts out another,
Or as one nail by strength drives out another,
Or just as one nail knocks out another by force,
So the remembrance of my former love
So the memory of my former love
Is by a newer object quite forgotten.
Is forgotten as a never love takes it's place.
Is it mine, or Valentine's praise,
Is it my praise, or Valentine's,
Her true perfection, or my false transgression,
Or her actual perfection, or me breaking my loyalty,
That makes me reasonless to reason thus?
That makes me think like this without a cause?
She is fair; and so is Julia that I love—

She is pretty, and is Julia who I love—
That I did love, for now my love is thaw'd;
Who I used to love, for now that lave has melted away;
Which, like a waxen image, 'gainst a fire,
And, like a figure made from wax, when held near a fire,
Bears no impression of the thing it was.
Looks nothing like the thing it used to be.
Methinks my zeal to Valentine is cold,
It seems to me that my loyalty to Valentine has gone stale,
And that I love him not as I was wont.
And that I don't love him as I used to.
O, but I love his lady too too much,
Oh, but I love his lady way too much,
And that's the reason I love him so little.
And that is why I love him so little.
How shall I dote on her with more advice,
How will I give adoring her more thought,
That thus without advice begin to love her!
When I began to love her without thinking!
'Tis but her picture I have yet beheld,
I have only seen her appearance,
And that hath dazzled my reason's light;
And that has stunned my ability to reason;
But when I look on her perfections,
But when I look later at her perfect qualities of character,
There is no reason but I shall be blind.
There is no doubt that I will be blind.
If I can cheque my erring love, I will;
If I can restrain my wrongful love, I will;
If not, to compass her I'll use my skill.
But if not, I will use my skill to win her over.

Exit

SCENE V. The same.

A street.

Enter SPEED and LAUNCE severally

SPEED
Launce! by mine honesty, welcome to Milan!
Launce! I swear by my own honesty, welcome to Milan!

LAUNCE
Forswear not thyself, sweet youth, for I am not
Don't swear against yourself, sweet young man, for I am not
welcome. I reckon this always, that a man is never
Welcome. I always believe this, that a man is never
undone till he be hanged, nor never welcome to a
Destroyed until he is executed, nor is he ever welcome to a
place till some certain shot be paid and the hostess
Place until his bill is paid and the hostess
say 'Welcome!'
Says 'Welcome!'

SPEED
Come on, you madcap, I'll to the alehouse with you
Come one, you lunatic, I'll go with you to the pub
presently; where, for one shot of five pence, thou
Immedieately; where, for a bill of five pennies, you
shalt have five thousand welcomes. But, sirrah, how
Will have five thousand welcomes. But, man, how
did thy master part with Madam Julia?
Did you master part ways with Madam Julia?

LAUNCE
Marry, after they closed in earnest, they parted very
By Mary, after they seriously embraced, they parted very
fairly in jest.
Kindly.

SPEED
But shall she marry him?
But will she marry him?

LAUNCE
No.
No.

SPEED
How then? shall he marry her?
What then? Will he marry her?

LAUNCE
No, neither.
No, not that either.

SPEED
What, are they broken?
What then, have they broken up?

LAUNCE
No, they are both as whole as a fish.
No, they are still as together as they ever were.

SPEED
Why, then, how stands the matter with them?
Well, then, what's the deal with them?

LAUNCE
Marry, thus: when it stands well with him, it
By Mary, it's like this: when it goes well with him, it
stands well with her.
Goes well with her.

SPEED
What an ass art thou! I understand thee not.
You're such an ass! I don't understand you.

LAUNCE
What a block art thou, that thou canst not! My
You're such a blockhead, that you can't undestand me! Even my
staff understands me.
Walking stick and stand under me.

SPEED
What thou sayest?
What are you saying?

LAUNCE

Ay, and what I do too: look thee, I'll but lean,
Yes, and it's what I do too: look here, I'll just lean,
and my staff understands me.
And my staff stand under me and holds my weight.

SPEED

It stands under thee, indeed.
It does stand under you, indeed.

LAUNCE

Why, stand-under and under-stand is all one.
Well, stand under and understand are the same thing.

SPEED

But tell me true, will't be a match?
But tell me honestly, will they get married.

LAUNCE

Ask my dog: if he say ay, it will! if he say no,
Ask my dog: if he says yes, they well! If he says no,
it will; if he shake his tail and say nothing, it will.
They will; the she wags his tail and says nothing, they will.

SPEED

The conclusion is then that it will.
So the conclusion is that they will get married.

LAUNCE

Thou shalt never get such a secret from me but by a parable.
I will never tell you such a secret from me unless it's indirectly.

SPEED

'Tis well that I get it so. But, Launce, how sayest
It's a good thing I get it then. But, Launce, what do you
thou, that my master is become a notable lover?
Say about how your master has become well known as a lover?

LAUNCE

I never knew him otherwise.
I've never known him to be different.

SPEED

Than how?
How so?

LAUNCE
A notable lubber, as thou reportest him to be.
A well-known lubbering idiot, as you say he is.

SPEED
Why, thou whoreson ass, thou mistakest me.
Why, you son of a whore! you ass! you misunderstood me.

LAUNCE
Why, fool, I meant not thee; I meant thy master.
Well, fool, I didn't mean you; I meant your master.

SPEED
I tell thee, my master is become a hot lover.
I tell you, my master has become a passionate lover.

LAUNCE
Why, I tell thee, I care not though he burn himself
Well, I tell you, I don't care if he burns himself
in love. If thou wilt, go with me to the alehouse;
with love. If you will, come with to the pub;
if not, thou art an Hebrew, a Jew, and not worth the
If not, then you are a Jew, and not worthy to be
name of a Christian.
Called a Christian.

SPEED
Why?
Why?

LAUNCE
Because thou hast not so much charity in thee as to
Because you don't have enough good will in you to
go to the ale with a Christian. Wilt thou go?
Go to the pub with a Christian. Will you come?

SPEED
At thy service.
I'm at your service.

Exeunt

SCENE VI. The same.

The DUKE'S palace.

Enter PROTEUS

PROTEUS
To leave my Julia, shall I be forsworn;
If I leave my dear Julia, I will have broken my oath of loyalty;
To love fair Silvia, shall I be forsworn;
If I love the beautiful Silvia, I will have broken my oath;
To wrong my friend, I shall be much forsworn;
If I commit and offence against my friend, I will have really broken my loyalty;
And even that power which gave me first my oath
And the same power of love, which provoked this first oath of loyalty
Provokes me to this threefold perjury;
Now provokes me to break my oath in three ways;
Love bade me swear and Love bids me forswear.
Love made me promise, and love makes me break my promise.
O sweet-suggesting Love, if thou hast sinned,
Oh irresistible Love, if you have ever sinned,
Teach me, thy tempted subject, to excuse it!
Teach me, your follower who is tempted to sin, to justify it!
At first I did adore a twinkling star,
First, I adored a woman who was like a twinkling star,
But now I worship a celestial sun.
But now I worship a woman who is like a heavenly sun.
Unheedful vows may heedfully be broken,
Careless promises can be carefully broken,
And he wants wit that wants resolved will
And a man lacks intelligence if he lacks the determined will
To learn his wit to exchange the bad for better.
To teach his mind to exchange bad thing for better things.
Fie, fie, unreverend tongue! to call her bad,
Shame, shame on you, you disrespectful tongue! To call her bad,
Whose sovereignty so oft thou hast preferr'd
Whose great excellence you chose so often
With twenty thousand soul-confirming oaths.
With twenty-thousand promises from your soul.
I cannot leave to love, and yet I do;

I cannot stop loving, but I have;
But there I leave to love where I should love.
But I have stopped loving where I should love.
Julia I lose and Valentine I lose:
I lose Julia and I lose Valentine:
If I keep them, I needs must lose myself;
If I keep them, I must lose myself.
If I lose them, thus find I by their loss
But if I lose them, I then find myself due to their loss
For Valentine myself, for Julia Silvia.
Myself in exchange for Valentine, and Silvia in exchange for Julia.
I to myself am dearer than a friend,
I am more dear to myself then a friend is,
For love is still most precious in itself;
For love is always very precious by it's nature;
And Silvia--witness Heaven, that made her fair!—
And Silvia—Heaven, which made her beautiful, bear witness!—
Shows Julia but a swarthy Ethiope.
Shows up Julia, who is merely like an unattractive Ethiopian.
I will forget that Julia is alive,
I will forget that Julia is alive,
Remembering that my love to her is dead;
As I will remember that my love for her is dead;
And Valentine I'll hold an enemy,
And I'll consider Valentine my enemy,
Aiming at Silvia as a sweeter friend.
And I'll aim to have Silvia as my sweet lover.
I cannot now prove constant to myself,
Now, I can't prove to be loyal to myself,
Without some treachery used to Valentine.
Without some betrayal against Valentine.
This night he meaneth with a corded ladder
Tonight he intends, using a rope ladder,
To climber celestial Silvia's chamber-window,
To climb to heavenly Silvia's bedroom window,
Myself in counsel, his competitor.
In confidence he told me this, his rival.
Now presently I'll give her father notice
Right now I'll warn her father
Of their disguising and pretended flight;
Of their intended deceptive escape;
Who, all enraged, will banish Valentine;
He will, being enraged, banish Valentine;
For Thurio, he intends, shall wed his daughter;

Since he intends that Thurio will marry his daughter;
But, Valentine being gone, I'll quickly cross
But, with Valentine gone, I'll quickly prevent this
By some sly trick blunt Thurio's dull proceeding.
With some clever trick to block dull-witted Thurio's advancement.
Love, lend me wings to make my purpose swift,
Love, give me winds to carry out my plan quickly,
As thou hast lent me wit to plot this drift!
Just as you have given me the intelligence to plot this plan.

Exit

SCENE VII. Verona.

JULIA'S house.

Enter JULIA and LUCETTA

JULIA
Counsel, Lucetta; gentle girl, assist me;
Give me some advice, Lucette; friendly girl, help me;
And even in kind love I do conjure thee,
And in the name of that same kind friendship, I entreat you,
Who art the table wherein all my thoughts
Who serve as the notebook in which all my thoughts
Are visibly character'd and engraved,
Are visibly written out,
To lesson me and tell me some good mean
To instruct me and tell me some good way
How, with my honour, I may undertake
That I can maintain my honor and go on
A journey to my loving Proteus.
A journey to my lover Proteus.

LUCETTA
Alas, the way is wearisome and long!
Sadly, that journey would be difficult and long!

JULIA
A true-devoted pilgrim is not weary
An honestly devoted follower is not exhausted
To measure kingdoms with his feeble steps;
By travelling through kingdoms with little steps;
Much less shall she that hath Love's wings to fly,
Much less will a woman who has the wing's of Love to fly on,
And when the flight is made to one so dear,
And when the journey is made to go to one who is so dear,
Of such divine perfection, as Sir Proteus.
And made of such holy perfection as is Sir Proteus.

LUCETTA
Better forbear till Proteus make return.
It would be better for you to be patient for Proteus' return.

JULIA

O, know'st thou not his looks are my soul's food?
Oh, don't you know that the looks he give me feed my soul?
Pity the dearth that I have pined in,
You should pity the lack of them that has caused me to ache,
By longing for that food so long a time.
In the same way the one aches for food after a long time.
Didst thou but know the inly touch of love,
If you only the heartfelt touch of love,
Thou wouldst as soon go kindle fire with snow
You would just as soon try to burn a fire with snow
As seek to quench the fire of love with words.
As to seek to put out the fire of love with words.

LUCETTA

I do not seek to quench your love's hot fire,
I'm not trying to put out your love's hot fire,
But qualify the fire's extreme rage,
But moderate the fire's extreme passion,
Lest it should burn above the bounds of reason.
So that it doesn't burn beyond the edges of reason.

JULIA

The more thou damm'st it up, the more it burns.
The more you try to stop it, the more it burns.
The current that with gentle murmur glides,
The current of a stream that gently flows,
Thou know'st, being stopp'd, impatiently doth rage;
You know, when it is stopped, eagerly turns rapid;
But when his fair course is not hindered,
But when its gentle course is not blocked,
He makes sweet music with the enamell'd stones,
It babbles over the smoothed stones,
Giving a gentle kiss to every sedge
Gentling touching every reed
He overtaketh in his pilgrimage,
It has passed over in its travels,
And so by many winding nooks he strays
And so it flows by route of many twisting corners
With willing sport to the wild ocean.
With prepared entertainment all the way to the wild ocean.
Then let me go and hinder not my course

Just like that, let me go and don't block my course
I'll be as patient as a gentle stream
And I'll be as patient as a gentle stream
And make a pastime of each weary step,
And make each tiring step into a game,
Till the last step have brought me to my love;
Until the last step has brought me to my love;
And there I'll rest, as after much turmoil
And there I will finally rest, just as after much chaos
A blessed soul doth in Elysium.
A blessed soul rests in Heaven.

LUCETTA
But in what habit will you go along?
But what will you wear on your journey?

JULIA
Not like a woman; for I would prevent
Not women's clothe; since I want to precent
The loose encounters of lascivious men:
Any improper meetings of lustful men:
Gentle Lucetta, fit me with such weeds
Kind Lucetta, dress me with clothes
As may beseem some well-reputed page.
That are fitting for a well-respected page.

LUCETTA
Why, then, your ladyship must cut your hair.
Well, then, you must cut your hair, my lady

JULIA
No, girl, I'll knit it up in silken strings
No, girl, I'll tie it up with silk strings
With twenty odd-conceited true-love knots.
With twenty ingeniously devised knots for true-love.
To be fantastic may become a youth
To be imaginative may be appropriate for a young person
Of greater time than I shall show to be.
Of more years than I will appear to be.

LUCETTA
What fashion, madam shall I make your breeches?
In what style should I make your breeches, madam?

JULIA

That fits as well as 'Tell me, good my lord,
That questions makes as much sense as 'Tell me, my good lord,
What compass will you wear your farthingale?'
What size hooped petticoat do you wear?'
Why even what fashion thou best likest, Lucetta.
Why, what ever style you like best, Lucette.

LUCETTA

You must needs have them with a codpiece, madam.
You must have breeches with a codpiece, madam.

JULIA

Out, out, Lucetta! that would be ill-favour'd.
Get out, Lucetta! That would be ugly.

LUCETTA

A round hose, madam, now's not worth a pin,
Puffy breeches, madam, are now not worth anything,
Unless you have a codpiece to stick pins on.
Unless you have a codpiece to decorate.

JULIA

Lucetta, as thou lovest me, let me have
Lucette, if you love me, give me
What thou thinkest meet and is most mannerly.
Whatever you think is fitting and is most appropriate.
But tell me, wench, how will the world repute me
But tell me, girl, what will the world think about me
For undertaking so unstaid a journey?
For embarking on such an unseemly journey?
I fear me, it will make me scandalized.
I'm afraid I will be disgraced.

LUCETTA

If you think so, then stay at home and go not.
If you think that will happen, then stay at home and don't go.

JULIA

Nay, that I will not.
No, I won't do that.

LUCETTA

Then never dream on infamy, but go.

Then don't think about a terrible reputation, just go.
If Proteus like your journey when you come,
If Proteus is pleased with your journey when you get there,
No matter who's displeased when you are gone:
I doesn't matter who doesn't like that you are gone:
I fear me, he will scarce be pleased withal.
I'm afraid that he won't be pleased with it.

JULIA
That is the least, Lucetta, of my fear:
That is the smallest of my fears, Lucetta:
A thousand oaths, an ocean of his tears
A thousand promises, an ocean of his tears
And instances of infinite of love
And infinite evidence of love
Warrant me welcome to my Proteus.
Assure me that Proteus will welcome me.

LUCETTA
All these are servants to deceitful men.
Dishonest men use all the techniques you just named.

JULIA
Base men, that use them to so base effect!
Dishonorable men that use them for such a dishonorable reason!
But truer stars did govern Proteus' birth
But more honest stars did rule over Proteus' birth;
His words are bonds, his oaths are oracles,
His words are binding promises, his oaths tell the truth,
His love sincere, his thoughts immaculate,
His love is sincere, his thoughts are untainted,
His tears pure messengers sent from his heart,
His tears are pure messengers sent from his heart,
His heart as far from fraud as heaven from earth.
His heart is as far from dishonesty as heaven is from earth.

LUCETTA
Pray heaven he prove so, when you come to him!
I pray to heaven that he proves to be honest when you get to him!

JULIA
Now, as thou lovest me, do him not that wrong
Now, if you love me, don't commit that unkindness against him
To bear a hard opinion of his truth:

That holding that poor opinion of his sincereity:
Only deserve my love by loving him;
You should only justify my love by loving him as well;
And presently go with me to my chamber,
And now come with me to me room,
To take a note of what I stand in need of,
To make a list of what I still need
To furnish me upon my longing journey.
To equip myself for my long journey.
All that is mine I leave at thy dispose,
All that I own, I leave in your control,
My goods, my lands, my reputation;
My goods, my lands, my reputation;
Only, in lieu thereof, dispatch me hence.
Just, in exchange for that, send me there.
Come, answer not, but to it presently!
Come on, don't answer me, just do it right away!
I am impatient of my tarriance.
I am impatient to delay.

Exeunt

ACT III

SCENE I. Milan.

The DUKE's palace.

Enter DUKE, THURIO, and PROTEUS

DUKE
Sir Thurio, give us leave, I pray, awhile;
Sir Thurio, give us some space, please, for a little while;
We have some secrets to confer about.
We have some secrets to talk about.

Exit THURIO

Now, tell me, Proteus, what's your will with me?
Now, tell me , Proteus, what is it you want with me?

PROTEUS
My gracious lord, that which I would discover
My gracious lord, the secret that I've come to tell you
The law of friendship bids me to conceal;
Is one that the law of friendship begs me to hide;
But when I call to mind your gracious favours
But when I think of the great favors you have
Done to me, undeserving as I am,
Done for me, even though I am unworthy,
My duty pricks me on to utter that
My sense of duty urges me to tell you the secret that
Which else no worldly good should draw from me.
No other mortal man would be able to get out of me.
Know, worthy prince, Sir Valentine, my friend,
Be aware, worthy duke, that my friend, Sir Valentine,
This night intends to steal away your daughter:
Intends to steal away your daughter tonight:
Myself am one made privy to the plot.
I was made aware of the plot in secret.
I know you have determined to bestow her
I know you have decided to give her hand in marriage
On Thurio, whom your gentle daughter hates;
To Thurio, a man who your noble daughter hates;
And should she thus be stol'n away from you,

And if she was stolen away from you like this,
It would be much vexation to your age.
It would be very distressing at your age.
Thus, for my duty's sake, I rather chose
So, because of my duty, I chose
To cross my friend in his intended drift
To betray my friend's intended plan
Than, by concealing it, heap on your head
Instead of, by keeping it secret, loading your heart with
A pack of sorrows which would press you down,
A bundle of grief that would weigh you down
Being unprevented, to your timeless grave.
Into your premature grave, if it was not prevented.

DUKE
Proteus, I thank thee for thine honest care;
Proteus, thank you for your honest concern;
Which to requite, command me while I live.
Which I will reward by allowing you to ask any favor from me while I live,
This love of theirs myself have often seen,
I have often seen this love of theirs,
Haply when they have judged me fast asleep,
When they perhaps thought that I was fast asleep,
And oftentimes have purposed to forbid
And often I have planned to forbid
Sir Valentine her company and my court:
Sir Valentine from being in her company or in my court:
But fearing lest my jealous aim might err
But I was afraid that my suspicious guess might be wrong
And so unworthily disgrace the man,
And in doing so I would mistakenly dishonor the man,
A rashness that I ever yet have shunn'd,
Which is a fool act that I have always avoided;
I gave him gentle looks, thereby to find
I looked at him kindly, in order to find out
That which thyself hast now disclosed to me.
What you have just revealed to me.
And, that thou mayst perceive my fear of this,
And, so that you can see how I have been afraid of this,
Knowing that tender youth is soon suggested,
Since I know that inexperienced youth is easy to tempt,
I nightly lodge her in an upper tower,
Every night I keep her in a high tower,
The key whereof myself have ever kept;

Whose key I always keep myself;
And thence she cannot be convey'd away.
So that she cannot be stolen away.

PROTEUS
Know, noble lord, they have devised a mean
Be aware, noble lord, that they have come up with a plan
How he her chamber-window will ascend
For him to climb up to her bedroom window
And with a corded ladder fetch her down;
Using a rope ladder and carry her down;
For which the youthful lover now is gone
Which the young lover has now to get
And this way comes he with it presently;
And will come back here with it soon;
Where, if it please you, you may intercept him.
Where, if you wanted, you could intercept him.
But, good my Lord, do it so cunningly
But, my good Lord, do it so cleverly
That my discovery be not aimed at;
That he won't guess that I've told you of it;
For love of you, not hate unto my friend,
Because it was my admiration of you, not hatred against my friend,
Hath made me publisher of this pretence.
That made me expose his plan.

DUKE
Upon mine honour, he shall never know
I swear on my honor that he will never know
That I had any light from thee of this.
That I had any information from you about this.

PROTEUS
Adieu, my Lord; Sir Valentine is coming.
Farewell, my Lord; Sir Valentine is coming.

Exit

Enter VALENTINE

DUKE
Sir Valentine, whither away so fast?
Sir Valentine, where are you going so quickly?

VALENTINE
Please it your grace, there is a messenger
If you would like to know, your grace, there is a messenger
That stays to bear my letters to my friends,
That is waiting to carry letters to my friends,
And I am going to deliver them.
And I am going to give them to him.

DUKE
Be they of much import?
Are they very important?

VALENTINE
The tenor of them doth but signify
The content of them only tells of
My health and happy being at your court.
My healthy and happy life in your court.

DUKE
Nay then, no matter; stay with me awhile;
No then, they're unimportant; stay here with me for a little while;
I am to break with thee of some affairs
I am going to tell you of some happenings
That touch me near, wherein thou must be secret.
That seriously concern me, which you must keep secret.
'Tis not unknown to thee that I have sought
It's well known to you that I am trying to
To match my friend Sir Thurio to my daughter.
To marry my friend Sir Thurio to my daughter.

VALENTINE
I know it well, my Lord; and, sure, the match
I know that well, my Lord; and, be sure, that match
Were rich and honourable; besides, the gentleman
Would be rich and honorable; besides, the gentleman
Is full of virtue, bounty, worth and qualities
Is very virtuous, generous, worthy and has many qualities
Beseeming such a wife as your fair daughter:
Fitting for such a wife as your beautiful daughter:
Cannot your Grace win her to fancy him?
Can't you get her to admire him, you grace?

DUKE
No, trust me; she is peevish, sullen, froward,

No, believe me; she is obstinate, angry, willful,
Proud, disobedient, stubborn, lacking duty,
Proud, disobedient, stubborn, and without a sense of duty,
Neither regarding that she is my child
Not respecting that she is my child
Nor fearing me as if I were her father;
Or being afraid of me since I am her father;
And, may I say to thee, this pride of hers,
And, if I can say this to you, this pride of hers,
Upon advice, hath drawn my love from her;
After serious thought, has made me not love her;
And, where I thought the remnant of mine age
And, where before I thought last of my days
Should have been cherish'd by her child-like duty,
Would be treasured by her since she is my child,
I now am full resolved to take a wife
I have now decided to take myself a wife
And turn her out to who will take her in:
And turn out my daughter to whoever will take her in:
Then let her beauty be her wedding-dower;
Then her beauty can we her dowry;
For me and my possessions she esteems not.
Since he doesn't respect me or my possessions.

VALENTINE
What would your Grace have me to do in this?
What would you like me to do about this, your grace?

DUKE
There is a lady in Verona here
There is a lady in here in Verona
Whom I affect; but she is nice and coy
Whom I love; but she is reluctant and distant
And nought esteems my aged eloquence:
And doesn't respect my old talk of love:
Now therefore would I have thee to my tutor—
So I would like for you to be my teacher—
For long agone I have forgot to court;
Since I have forgot a long time ago how to pursue a woman;
Besides, the fashion of the time is changed—
Besides, the style of the time has changed—
How and which way I may bestow myself
How and in what way can I behave
To be regarded in her sun-bright eye.

So that I can well regarded in her sunny eyes.

VALENTINE
Win her with gifts, if she respect not words:
Win her over with gifts, if she doesn't pay attention your words:
Dumb jewels often in their silent kind
Mute jewels by their silent nature
More than quick words do move a woman's mind.
Change a woman's mind quicker than words.

DUKE
But she did scorn a present that I sent her.
But she belittled a present that I sent her.

VALENTINE
A woman sometimes scorns what best contents her.
A woman sometimes will belittle what makes her the most happy.
Send her another; never give her o'er;
Send her another gift; never give up on her;
For scorn at first makes after-love the more.
Since her initial contempt will make her later love all the greater.
If she do frown, 'tis not in hate of you,
If she frowns, it's not because she hates you,
But rather to beget more love in you:
But rather to make you love her more:
If she do chide, 'tis not to have you gone;
If she scolds you, it's not so that you will go away;
For why, the fools are mad, if left alone.
Because foolish women go crazy if they are left alone.
Take no repulse, whatever she doth say;
Don't take any rejections, whatever she may say;
For 'get you gone,' she doth not mean 'away!'
For 'go away,' she doesn't really mean 'away!'
Flatter and praise, commend, extol their graces;
Flatter and praise her, admire, commend her virtues;
Though ne'er so black, say they have angels' faces.
No matter how unattractive tell her she has the face of an angel.
That man that hath a tongue, I say, is no man,
I say that a man with words is no man at all
If with his tongue he cannot win a woman.
If his words cannot win over a woman.

DUKE
But she I mean is promised by her friends

But her hand in marriage has been promised by her family
Unto a youthful gentleman of worth,
To a young gentlemen of importance,
And kept severely from resort of men,
And she is strictly kept away from visits from other men,
That no man hath access by day to her.
So that no man can see her during the day.

VALENTINE
Why, then, I would resort to her by night.
Well, then, I would visit her by night.

DUKE
Ay, but the doors be lock'd and keys kept safe,
Yes, but the doors are locked and the keys are kept safe,
That no man hath recourse to her by night.
So that no man has access to her at night.

VALENTINE
What lets but one may enter at her window?
What is to prevent someone form entering from her window?

DUKE
Her chamber is aloft, far from the ground,
Her bedroom is up high, far from the ground,
And built so shelving that one cannot climb it
And built with an overhang so that no one can climb it
Without apparent hazard of his life.
Without certainly endangering his life.

VALENTINE
Why then, a ladder quaintly made of cords,
Well then, a ladder skillfully made of rope,
To cast up, with a pair of anchoring hooks,
To toss up, with a pair of anchoring hooks,
Would serve to scale another Hero's tower,
Would work to climb this tower that is like Hero's tower,
So bold Leander would adventure it.
If you would be like Hero's Leander, and risk climbing it.

DUKE
Now, as thou art a gentleman of blood,
Now, since you are a spirited gentleman
Advise me where I may have such a ladder.

Tell me where I may find a ladder like that.

VALENTINE
When would you use it? pray, sir, tell me that.
When would you use it? Please, tell me that, sir.

DUKE
This very night; for Love is like a child,
Tonight; because Love is like a child
That longs for every thing that he can come by.
That desires everything he can get.

VALENTINE
By seven o'clock I'll get you such a ladder.
By seven o'clock I can get you a ladder like that

DUKE
But, hark thee; I will go to her alone:
But, listen; I will be going to her alone:
How shall I best convey the ladder thither?
What is the best way to carry the ladder there?

VALENTINE
It will be light, my lord, that you may bear it
It won't be heavy, my lord, so that you can carry it
Under a cloak that is of any length.
Under a clock if the cloak is a bit long.

DUKE
A cloak as long as thine will serve the turn?
A cloak as long as yours will work for that?

VALENTINE
Ay, my good lord.
Yes, my good lord.

DUKE
Then let me see thy cloak:
Then let me see your cloak:
I'll get me one of such another length.
I'll get myself one of the same length.

VALENTINE
Why, any cloak will serve the turn, my lord.

Well, any cloak will work for the purpose, my lord.

DUKE
How shall I fashion me to wear a cloak?
How will I get myself used to to wearing a cloak?
I pray thee, let me feel thy cloak upon me.
Please, let me try on your cloak.

"[DUKE opens VALENTINE's cloak and finds the rope ladder and a letter]"

What letter is this same? What's here? 'To Silvia'!
What is this letter here? What's written here? 'To Silvia'!
And here an engine fit for my proceeding.
And here is the tool fit for my plan of action.
I'll be so bold to break the seal for once.
I'll overstep my place and break the seal just this once.

Reads

'My thoughts do harbour with my Silvia nightly,
'My thoughts are all about Silvia every night,
And slaves they are to me that send them flying:
And they are like my slaves that I send flying off to her:
O, could their master come and go as lightly,
Oh, if only I, their master, could come and go as easily,
Himself would lodge where senseless they are lying!
I would stay there with her where my thoughts lie down being unaware!
My herald thoughts in thy pure bosom rest them:
My thoughts are messengers that rest in your pure heart:
While I, their king, that hither them importune,
While I, their master, who urged them to go to you,
Do curse the grace that with such grace hath bless'd them,
Curse their success that they have been blessed with such an honor,
Because myself do want my servants' fortune:
Because I want my servant's good fortune for myself:
I curse myself, for they are sent by me,
I curse myself, because they were sent by me,
That they should harbour where their lord would be.'
And they are able to rest where their master should be.'
What's here?
What's this all about?
'Silvia, this night I will enfranchise thee.'
'Silvia, tonight I will set you free.'
'Tis so; and here's the ladder for the purpose.

It's true; and here's the ladder to do it with.
Why, Phaeton,--for thou art Merops' son,--
Why, Phaeton—because I will call you that since you are like Merops' son in myth—
Wilt thou aspire to guide the heavenly car
Do you also seek to drive the sun's chariot
And with thy daring folly burn the world?
And because of your brave foolishness burn the whole world?
Wilt thou reach stars, because they shine on thee?
Would you fly up to the stars just because they shine down on you?
Go, base intruder! overweening slave!
Go away, you dishonorable burglar! You arrogant scoundrel!
Bestow thy fawning smiles on equal mates,
Give your flirting smiles to women who are of your same social rank,
And think my patience, more than thy desert,
And consider my patience with you, which was more than you deserved,
Is privilege for thy departure hence:
To be a privilege for allowing you to simply leave here:
Thank me for this more than for all the favours
Thank me for this more than you thank me for all the other favors
Which all too much I have bestow'd on thee.
That I have give to you all too often.
But if thou linger in my territories
But if you stay in my lands
Longer than swiftest expedition
For longer than it takes for the quickest departure
Will give thee time to leave our royal court,
That still gives you enough time to leave my royal court,
By heaven! my wrath shall far exceed the love
By heaven! My wrath will by far surpass the love
I ever bore my daughter or thyself.
I ever had for my daughter or for you.
Be gone! I will not hear thy vain excuse;
Be gone! I won't listen to your useless excuse;
But, as thou lovest thy life, make speed from hence.
Only, if you value your life, get away from here quickly.

Exit

VALENTINE
And why not death rather than living torment?
And why is death not better than living in torture?
To die is to be banish'd from myself;
To die means to be exiled from myself;
And Silvia is myself: banish'd from her

92

And Silvia is the same as myself: being exiled from her
Is self from self: a deadly banishment!
Is the same as being exiled from myself: a deadly exile!
What light is light, if Silvia be not seen?
What light is still light, if I can't see Silvia?
What joy is joy, if Silvia be not by?
What joy is still joy, if Silvia is not nearby?
Unless it be to think that she is by
Unless it is just so that I think she is nearby
And feed upon the shadow of perfection.
And take pleasure in the illusion of her perfect presence.
Except I be by Silvia in the night,
Unless I am with Silvia at night,
There is no music in the nightingale;
There is no music in the nightingale's song;
Unless I look on Silvia in the day,
Unless I look at Silvia during the day,
There is no day for me to look upon;
There isn't a day that is really a day for me to see at all;
She is my essence, and I leave to be,
She is my very life, and I will stop existing,
If I be not by her fair influence
If her beautiful power doesn't
Foster'd, illumined, cherish'd, kept alive.
Care for me, light me up, treasure me, and keep me alive.
I fly not death, to fly his deadly doom:
I am not escaping death by escaping the duke's deadly sentence:
Tarry I here, I but attend on death:
If I stay here, I am only waiting for death:
But, fly I hence, I fly away from life.
But if I escape from here, I am escaping from life.

Enter PROTEUS and LAUNCE

PROTEUS
Run, boy, run, run, and seek him out.
Run, boy, run, run, and find him.

LAUNCE
Soho, soho!
Tally-ho!

PROTEUS
What seest thou?

What do you see?

LAUNCE
Him we go to find: there's not a hair on's head
I see the man we're trying to find: there's not a hair on his head
but 'tis a Valentine.
Unless this is Valentine.

PROTEUS
Valentine?
Valentine?

VALENTINE
No.
I'm not Valentine.

PROTEUS
Who then? his spirit?
Who are you then? His ghost?

VALENTINE
Neither.
Not that either.

PROTEUS
What then?
Who are you then?

VALENTINE
Nothing.
I am nothing.

LAUNCE
Can nothing speak? Master, shall I strike?
And nothing is able to speak? Master, should I hit him?

PROTEUS
Who wouldst thou strike?
Who would you hit?

LAUNCE
Nothing.
Nothing.

PROTEUS
Villain, forbear.
You scoundrel, stop it.

LAUNCE
Why, sir, I'll strike nothing: I pray you,--
Well, sir, I'll hit nothing: please—

PROTEUS
Sirrah, I say, forbear. Friend Valentine, a word.
Man, I said, stop it. My friend Valentine, I would like to speak with you.

VALENTINE
My ears are stopt and cannot hear good news,
My ears are stopped up and cannot hear good news,
So much of bad already hath possess'd them.
Since so much bad news has already taken them over.

PROTEUS
Then in dumb silence will I bury mine,
Then I will relate my news in complete silence,
For they are harsh, untuneable and bad.
For it is harsh, terrible and bad.

VALENTINE
Is Silvia dead?
Is Silvia dead?

PROTEUS
No, Valentine.
No, Valentine.

VALENTINE
No Valentine, indeed, for sacred Silvia.
There will be no Valentine, indeed, for heavenly Silvia.
Hath she forsworn me?
Has she rejected me?

PROTEUS
No, Valentine.
No, Valentine.

VALENTINE
No Valentine, if Silvia have forsworn me.

There would be no more Valentine if Silvia rejected me.
What is your news?
What's your news?

LAUNCE
Sir, there is a proclamation that you are vanished.
Sir, there was a public announcement that you vanished.

PROTEUS
That thou art banished--O, that's the news!—
He means that your are banished—Oh, that's the news!—
From hence, from Silvia and from me thy friend.
From here, from Silvia, and from my your friend.

VALENTINE
O, I have fed upon this woe already,
Oh, I have found out this terrible news already,
And now excess of it will make me surfeit.
And now too much of it will make me be sick.
Doth Silvia know that I am banished?
Does Silvia know that I am banished?

PROTEUS
Ay, ay; and she hath offer'd to the doom—
Yes, yes; and she has responded to the sentence—
Which, unreversed, stands in effectual force—
Which, if it isn't reversed, is in full effect—
A sea of melting pearl, which some call tears:
With a stream of melted pearls, which some call tears:
Those at her father's churlish feet she tender'd;
She let those fall at her father's ugly feet;
With them, upon her knees, her humble self;
With her tears, and on her knees, she humiliated herself;
Wringing her hands, whose whiteness so became them
Wringing her hands, whose whiteness was so fitting for them
As if but now they waxed pale for woe:
That they seemed to turn pale from sadness;
But neither bended knees, pure hands held up,
But not her kneeling before him, or her pure hands held up to him,
Sad sighs, deep groans, nor silver-shedding tears,
Her sad signs, deep groans, nor tears of falling silver,
Could penetrate her uncompassionate sire;
Could break through to her uncaring father;
But Valentine, if he be ta'en, must die.

But Valentine will be killed, if you are taken in.
Besides, her intercession chafed him so,
Besides, her prayer for you angered him so much,
When she for thy repeal was suppliant,
When she was begging for your forgiveness,
That to close prison he commanded her,
That he sent her to a private prison,
With many bitter threats of biding there.
With many terrible threats of remaining there.

VALENTINE
No more; unless the next word that thou speak'st
Say no more; unless the next word that you speak
Have some malignant power upon my life:
Has some deadly power to end my life:
If so, I pray thee, breathe it in mine ear,
If it does, please, whisper it in my ear,
As ending anthem of my endless dolour.
As the last song of my endless grief.

PROTEUS
Cease to lament for that thou canst not help,
Stop grieving for what you cannot change,
And study help for that which thou lament'st.
And think of what you can do about what you're grieving for.
Time is the nurse and breeder of all good.
Time heals all wounds.
Here if thou stay, thou canst not see thy love;
If you stay here, you cannot see your love;
Besides, thy staying will abridge thy life.
Besides, if you stay you will cut your life short.
Hope is a lover's staff; walk hence with that
A lover's walking stick is made of hope; walk from here with that
And manage it against despairing thoughts.
And use it against your thoughts of despair.
Thy letters may be here, though thou art hence;
Your letter will be here, though you are away;
Which, being writ to me, shall be deliver'd
Which, if you write them to me, I will deliver
Even in the milk-white bosom of thy love.
To the milky-white chest of your love.
The time now serves not to expostulate:
We don't have the time now to discuss:
Come, I'll convey thee through the city-gate;

Come on, I'll take you through the city-gate;
And, ere I part with thee, confer at large
And, before I part with you, discuss in full
Of all that may concern thy love-affairs.
Of everything that may concern your love affair.
As thou lovest Silvia, though not for thyself,
Since you love Silvia, even though you don't love yourself,
Regard thy danger, and along with me!
Take notice of your danger, and come along with me!

VALENTINE
I pray thee, Launce, an if thou seest my boy,
Please, Launce, if you see my servant boy,
Bid him make haste and meet me at the North-gate.
Tell him to hurry and meet me at the North-gate.

PROTEUS
Go, sirrah, find him out. Come, Valentine.
Go, man, find him. Come on, Valentine.

VALENTINE
O my dear Silvia! Hapless Valentine!
Oh, my dear Silvia! Miserable Valentine!

Exeunt VALENTINE and PROTEUS

LAUNCE
I am but a fool, look you; and yet I have the wit to
I am just a fool, you know; and still I have the sense to
think my master is a kind of a knave: but that's
Think my master is a kind of scoundrel: but that's
all one, if he be but one knave. He lives not now
Alright, if he's only a knave in this one instance. Not a man lives
that knows me to be in love; yet I am in love; but a
That knows that I am in love; but I am in love; anything less than a
team of horse shall not pluck that from me; nor who
Team of horses will not get that secret out of me; nor who
'tis I love; and yet 'tis a woman; but what woman, I
It is that I love; but I'll say she's a a woman; and what a woman she is, I
will not tell myself; and yet 'tis a milkmaid; yet
Won't even tell myself; but I'll say she's a milkmaid; but
'tis not a maid, for she hath had gossips; yet 'tis
She's not a virgin, for she has had children; but she is
a maid, for she is her master's maid, and serves for

A maid, because she is her master's maid, and works for
wages. She hath more qualities than a water-spaniel;
Pay. She has more accomplishments than a water-spaniel;
which is much in a bare Christian.
Which is a lot for a mere Christian.

Pulling out a paper

Here is the cate-log of her condition.
Here is the list of her qualities.
'Imprimis: She can fetch and carry.' Why, a horse
'In the first place: she can fetch and carry things.' Well, a horse
can do no more: nay, a horse cannot fetch, but only
Can't even do that: no, a horse can't fetch, but can only
carry; therefore is she better than a jade. 'Item:
Carry; so she is better than an old nag. 'Next point:
She can milk;' look you, a sweet virtue in a maid
She can milk a cow;' you know, which is a good ability in a maid
with clean hands.
With clean hands

Enter SPEED

SPEED
How now, Signior Launce! what news with your
How are you, Mister Launce! What news do you have of your
mastership?
Lordship?

LAUNCE
With my master's ship? why, it is at sea.
Of my lord's ship? Well, it's out at sea.

SPEED
Well, your old vice still; mistake the word. What
Well, always with your old bad habit of misunderstanding words. What's
news, then, in your paper?
That paper there say, then?

LAUNCE
The blackest news that ever thou heardest.
The blackest news that you have ever heard.

SPEED

Why, man, how black?
Why, man, is it so black?

LAUNCE
Why, as black as ink.
Well, as black as ink.

SPEED
Let me read them.
Let me read them.

LAUNCE
Fie on thee, jolt-head! thou canst not read.
Shame on you, blockhead! You can't read.

SPEED
Thou liest; I can.
You're lying; I can read.

LAUNCE
I will try thee. Tell me this: who begot thee?
I will test you. Tell me this: who gave birth to you?

SPEED
Marry, the son of my grandfather.
By Mary, it was the son of my grandfather.

LAUNCE
O illiterate loiterer! it was the son of thy
Oh, illiterate beggar! It was the son of your
grandmother: this proves that thou canst not read.
Grandmother: this proves that you can't read.

SPEED
Come, fool, come; try me in thy paper.
Come on, fool, come on; test me with your paper.

LAUNCE
There; and St. Nicholas be thy speed!
Here it is; and may St. Nicholas help you!

SPEED
[Reads] 'Imprimis: She can milk.'
[Reads] 'In the first place: She can milk a cow.'

LAUNCE
Ay, that she can.
Yes, that she can do.

SPEED
'Item: She brews good ale.'
'Next point: she makes good ale.'

LAUNCE
And thereof comes the proverb: 'Blessing of your
And from there comes the phrase: 'Love of your
heart, you brew good ale.'
Heart, you make good ale.'

SPEED
'Item: She can sew.'
'Next point: she can sew.'

LAUNCE
That's as much as to say, Can she so?
That could mean, 'Can she so?'

SPEED
'Item: She can knit.'
'Next point: she can knit.'

LAUNCE
What need a man care for a stock with a wench, when
What does a man need a dowry for from a girl, when
she can knit him a stock?
She can knit him a stocking?

SPEED
'Item: She can wash and scour.'
'Next point: she can wash and scrub.'

LAUNCE
A special virtue: for then she need not be washed
A special skill: because then she doesn't need to be washed
and scoured.
And scrubbed.

SPEED

'Item: She can spin.'
'Next point: she can spin thread.'

LAUNCE
Then may I set the world on wheels, when she can
Then I can have an easy life, since she can
spin for her living.
Spin thread for her living.

SPEED
'Item: She hath many nameless virtues.'
Next point: she has many skills beyond words.'

LAUNCE
That's as much as to say, bastard virtues; that,
That's could mean, illegitimate children; who,
indeed, know not their fathers and therefore have no names.
Indeed, don't know who their fathers are and so don't have any names.

SPEED
'Here follow her vices.'
'Here are listed her bad qualities.'

LAUNCE
Close at the heels of her virtues.
Right after he good qualities.

SPEED
'Item: She is not to be kissed fasting in respect
'Next point: she is not to be kissed if she hasn't eaten on account
of her breath.'
Of her breath.'

LAUNCE
Well, that fault may be mended with a breakfast. Read on.
Well, that imperfection can be fixed with a breakfast. Keep reading.

SPEED
'Item: She hath a sweet mouth.'
'Next point: she has a sweet tooth.'

LAUNCE
That makes amends for her sour breath.
That makes up for her bad breath.

SPEED
'Item: She doth talk in her sleep.'
Next point: she talks in her sleep.'

LAUNCE
It's no matter for that, so she sleep not in her talk.
That's not a problem, as long as she doesn't sleep while she talks.

SPEED
'Item: She is slow in words.'
Next point: she is slow with words.'

LAUNCE
O villain, that set this down among her vices! To
Oh, what a scoundrel is the man who wrote that down as a bad quality! To
be slow in words is a woman's only virtue: I pray
Be slow with words is a woman's only skill: Please,
thee, out with't, and place it for her chief virtue.
Cross that out, and list it as her best quality.

SPEED
'Item: She is proud.'
'Next point: she is high-spirited.'

LAUNCE
Out with that too; it was Eve's legacy, and cannot
Cross that out too; she inherited that from Eve of Eden, and that cannot
be ta'en from her.
Be taken away from her.

SPEED
'Item: She hath no teeth.'
'Next point: she doesn't have any teeth.'

LAUNCE
I care not for that neither, because I love crusts.
I don't care about that either, because I love eating the crusts.

SPEED
'Item: She is curst.'
Next point: she is bad-tempered.'

LAUNCE

Well, the best is, she hath no teeth to bite.
Well, then it's a good thing that she has no teeth to bite with.

SPEED

'Item: She will often praise her liquor.'
'Next point: she will often test out her liquor.'

LAUNCE

If her liquor be good, she shall: if she will not, I
If her liquor is good, she will; if she doesn't, then I
will; for good things should be praised.
Will; since good things should be tested.

SPEED

'Item: She is too liberal.'
'Next point: she is too generous.'

LAUNCE

Of her tongue she cannot, for that's writ down she
With her words she isn't, because it's written down that she
is slow of; of her purse she shall not, for that
Is slow with words; she won't be with her money, because that
I'll keep shut: now, of another thing she may, and
I'll keep shut: now, with anything else she is can be, and
that cannot I help. Well, proceed.
That I can't help. Well, continue.

SPEED

'Item: She hath more hair than wit, and more faults
Next point: she has more hair than she has intelligence, and more imperfections
than hairs, and more wealth than faults.'
Than hair, and more money than imperfections.'

LAUNCE

Stop there; I'll have her: she was mine, and not
Stop reading there; I'll take her: I wanted her and didn't
mine, twice or thrice in that last article.
Want her, two or three times in that last point.
Rehearse that once more.
Repeat that one again.

SPEED

'Item: She hath more hair than wit,'—
'Next point: she has more hair than intelligence,'—

LAUNCE

More hair than wit? It may be; I'll prove it. The
More hair than intelligence? That could be true; I'll prove it with logic. The
cover of the salt hides the salt, and therefore it
Container of the salt hides the salt, and therefore it
is more than the salt; the hair that covers the wit
Is bigger than the salt; the hair that covers over the intelligence
is more than the wit, for the greater hides the
Is more than the intelligence because the bigger thing hides the
less. What's next?
Smaller thing. What's next?

SPEED

'And more faults than hairs,'—
'And more imperfections than hairs,'—

LAUNCE

That's monstrous: O, that that were out!
That's outrageous: oh, I wish that were crossed out!

SPEED

'And more wealth than faults.'
'And more wealth than imperfections.'

LAUNCE

Why, that word makes the faults gracious. Well,
Well, those words make the imperfections delightful. Well,
I'll have her; and if it be a match, as nothing is
I'll take her; and if we are a good match, since nothing is
impossible,--
Impossible—

SPEED

What then?
What then?

LAUNCE

Why, then will I tell thee--that thy master stays
Well, then I will tell you—your master is waiting
for thee at the North-gate.
For you at the North-gate.

SPEED

For me?
For me?

LAUNCE
For thee! ay, who art thou? he hath stayed for a
For you! Yes, who do you think you are? He has waited for
better man than thee.
Better men than you.

SPEED
And must I go to him?
And I have to go to him?

LAUNCE
Thou must run to him, for thou hast stayed so long
You must run to him, because you have delayed so long
that going will scarce serve the turn.
That walking will barely get the job done.

SPEED
Why didst not tell me sooner? pox of your love letters!
Why didn't you tell me sooner? Curse your love letters!

Exit

LAUNCE
Now will he be swinged for reading my letter; an
Now he'll be beaten for reading my letter; a
unmannerly slave, that will thrust himself into
Scoundrel without manners, who forces himself into
secrets! I'll after, to rejoice in the boy's correction.
Secrets! I'll follow him, to celebrate the man's punishment.

Exit

SCENE II. The same.

The DUKE's palace.

Enter DUKE and THURIO

DUKE
Sir Thurio, fear not but that she will love you,
Sir Thurio, don't be afraid that she won't love you,
Now Valentine is banish'd from her sight.
Because now Valentine is forbidden to see her.

THURIO
Since his exile she hath despised me most,
She has hated me more since his exile,
Forsworn my company and rail'd at me,
Rejected my company and yelled at me,
That I am desperate of obtaining her.
So that I am hopeless of ever winning her over.

DUKE
This weak impress of love is as a figure
The weak impression of love is like a stature
Trenched in ice, which with an hour's heat
Cut from ice, which after being in the heat for an hour
Dissolves to water and doth lose his form.
Melts into water and loses its shape.
A little time will melt her frozen thoughts
A little time will melt her unchanging thoughts
And worthless Valentine shall be forgot.
And worthless Valentine will be forgotten.

Enter PROTEUS

How now, Sir Proteus! Is your countryman
How goes it, Sir Proteus! Is your friend from home
According to our proclamation gone?
Gone following our public announcement of his exile?

PROTEUS
Gone, my good lord.

He's gone, my good lord.

DUKE
My daughter takes his going grievously.
My daughter is taking his departure with much grief.

PROTEUS
A little time, my lord, will kill that grief.
A little time, my lord, will make that grief go away.

DUKE
So I believe; but Thurio thinks not so.
I think so too; but Thurio doesn't believe that.
Proteus, the good conceit I hold of thee—
Proteus, the good opinion I have of you—
For thou hast shown some sign of good desert—
Since you have shown signs of deserving a good opinion—
Makes me the better to confer with thee.
Makes me more willing to discuss with you.

PROTEUS
Longer than I prove loyal to your grace
If I no longer prove to be loyal to your grace
Let me not live to look upon your grace.
Don't let me live to look at you, your grace.

DUKE
Thou know'st how willingly I would effect
You know how eagerly I want to bring about
The match between Sir Thurio and my daughter.
The marriage between Sir Thurio and my daughter.

PROTEUS
I do, my lord.
I do, my lord.

DUKE
And also, I think, thou art not ignorant
And also, I think, you are aware of
How she opposes her against my will
How she resists my wish.

PROTEUS
She did, my lord, when Valentine was here.

She did, my lord, when Valentine was here.

DUKE
Ay, and perversely she persevers so.
Yes, and obstinately she persisted like that.
What might we do to make the girl forget
What can we do to make the girl forget
The love of Valentine and love Sir Thurio?
Her love of Valentine and love Sir Thurio instead?

PROTEUS
The best way is to slander Valentine
The best way is to start rumors about Valentine
With falsehood, cowardice and poor descent,
Being dishonest, cowardly, and from a poor family—
Three things that women highly hold in hate.
Three things that women look at with hate.

DUKE
Ay, but she'll think that it is spoke in hate.
Yes, but she'll think that it is spoken from hatred of him.

PROTEUS
Ay, if his enemy deliver it:
Yes, if his enemy start it;
Therefore it must with circumstance be spoken
That's why it must be said with an explanation
By one whom she esteemeth as his friend.
By one who she considers to be his friend.

DUKE
Then you must undertake to slander him.
Then you must take on the task of starting the rumors about him.

PROTEUS
And that, my lord, I shall be loath to do:
And that, my lord, I would be very reluctant to do:
'Tis an ill office for a gentleman,
It's a terrible task for a gentleman,
Especially against his very friend.
Especially against his own friend.

DUKE
Where your good word cannot advantage him,

If your good word cannot promote him,
Your slander never can endamage him;
Then your rumors can never damage him;
Therefore the office is indifferent,
So the task is neither good nor bad,
Being entreated to it by your friend.
Especially if you are asked to do it by me, your friend.

PROTEUS
You have prevail'd, my lord; if I can do it
You have won, my lord; if I can do it
By ought that I can speak in his dispraise,
With anything that I can say to bring him down,
She shall not long continue love to him.
She will not continue to love him for lon.
But say this weed her love from Valentine,
But even if this extinguishes her love for Valentine,
It follows not that she will love Sir Thurio.
This doesn't mean that she will love Sir Thurio.

THURIO
Therefore, as you unwind her love from him,
So, as you rid her of her love for him,
Lest it should ravel and be good to none,
So that it doesn't become confused and is of no good to anyone,
You must provide to bottom it on me;
You must concentrate it on me;
Which must be done by praising me as much
Which you can do by praising me as much
As you in worth dispraise Sir Valentine.
As you admirably bring down Sir Valentine.

DUKE
And, Proteus, we dare trust you in this kind,
And, Proteus, we have the courage to trust you with this business,
Because we know, on Valentine's report,
Because we know, from Valentine's description,
You are already Love's firm votary
That you are already a firm worshiper of Love
And cannot soon revolt and change your mind.
And won't resist and change your mind soon.
Upon this warrant shall you have access
With my authorization you will have access
Where you with Silvia may confer at large;

To a place where you and Silvia can talk at length;
For she is lumpish, heavy, melancholy,
Because she is dejected, sad, melancholy,
And, for your friend's sake, will be glad of you;
And will be happy for your company, for your friend's sake;
Where you may temper her by your persuasion
Then you can shape her by persuading her
To hate young Valentine and love my friend.
To hate young Valentine and love my friend Thurio.

PROTEUS
As much as I can do, I will effect:
I will produce as much as I can:
But you, Sir Thurio, are not sharp enough;
But you, Sir Thurio, are not passionate enough;
You must lay lime to tangle her desires
You must lay traps to catch her love
By wailful sonnets, whose composed rhymes
With mournful poems, whose written lines
Should be full-fraught with serviceable vows.
Should be jam-packed with vows of loyalty.

DUKE
Ay,
Yes,
Much is the force of heaven-bred poesy.
The force of heavenly poetry is great.

PROTEUS
Say that upon the altar of her beauty
Say that in worshiping her beauty
You sacrifice your tears, your sighs, your heart:
You have sacrificed your tears, your sighs, and your heart:
Write till your ink be dry, and with your tears
Write until your ink is dry, and then with your tears
Moist it again, and frame some feeling line
Wet the paper again, and write some heartfelt line
That may discover such integrity:
That may reveal such complete devotion:
For Orpheus' lute was strung with poets' sinews,
Because the famous lover Orpheus' lute had strings made from the flesh of poets,
Whose golden touch could soften steel and stones,
Whose precious musical skill could soften steel and stones,
Make tigers tame and huge leviathans

And make tigers times and huge sea monsters
Forsake unsounded deeps to dance on sands.
Leave the unmeasured deeps of the ocean to dance on the shore.
After your dire-lamenting elegies,
After your deeply mournful love poems,
Visit by night your lady's chamber-window
Visit your lady's bedroom window at night
With some sweet concert; to their instruments
With some sweet music; with the music instruments
Tune a deploring dump: the night's dead silence
Play a sorrowful song: the night's dead silence
Will well become such sweet-complaining grievance.
Will be very fitting for such a sweetly sounding pain.
This, or else nothing, will inherit her.
If this doesn't win her over, nothing else will.

DUKE
This discipline shows thou hast been in love.
This instructions shows that you have been in love

THURIO
And thy advice this night I'll put in practise.
And I'll put your advice into practice tonight.
Therefore, sweet Proteus, my direction-giver,
So, sweet Proteus, my guide,
Let us into the city presently
Let us go to the city right now
To sort some gentlemen well skill'd in music.
To find some gentlemen well skilled in music.
I have a sonnet that will serve the turn
I have a poem that will work for this
To give the onset to thy good advice.
To star acting on your good advice.

DUKE
About it, gentlemen!
Get to it, gentlemen!

PROTEUS
We'll wait upon your grace till after supper,
We'll wait with your grace until after supper,
And afterward determine our proceedings.
And afterwards determine how to proceed with the plan.

DUKE
Even now about it! I will pardon you.
Get to it now! I will forgive you for not waiting with me.

Exeunt

ACT IV

SCENE I. The frontiers of Mantua.

A forest.

Enter certain Outlaws

First Outlaw
Fellows, stand fast; I see a passenger.
Men, get ready; I see a traveler.

Second Outlaw
If there be ten, shrink not, but down with 'em.
If there are ten men, don't give in, but bring them all down.

Enter VALENTINE and SPEED

Third Outlaw
Stand, sir, and throw us that you have about ye:
Stop, sir, and throw us whatever you have on you:
If not: we'll make you sit and rifle you.
If you don't: we'll put you on the ground and rob you.

SPEED
Sir, we are undone; these are the villains
Sir, we are ruined; these are the criminals
That all the travellers do fear so much.
That all the travelers are so afraid of.

VALENTINE
My friends,--
My friends—

First Outlaw
That's not so, sir: we are your enemies.
We aren't your friends, sir: we are your enemies.

Second Outlaw
Peace! we'll hear him.
Quiet! Let's listen to him.

Third Outlaw

Ay, by my beard, will we, for he's a proper man.
Yeah, by my beard, we'll listen to him, because he's a handsome man.

VALENTINE
Then know that I have little wealth to lose:
Then be aware that I have very little money for your to take:
A man I am cross'd with adversity;
I am a man plagued by misfortune;
My riches are these poor habiliments,
My only riches are these poor clothes,
Of which if you should here disfurnish me,
And if you should strip me of these,
You take the sum and substance that I have.
You will be taking everything single thing that I have.

Second Outlaw
Whither travel you?
Where are you traveling to?

VALENTINE
To Verona.
To Verona.

First Outlaw
Whence came you?
Where did you come from?

VALENTINE
From Milan.
From Milan.

Third Outlaw
Have you long sojourned there?
How long were you staying here?

VALENTINE
Some sixteen months, and longer might have stay'd,
About sixteen months, and I might have stayed longer,
If crooked fortune had not thwarted me.
If tricky chance had not stood in my way.

First Outlaw
What, were you banish'd thence?
What, were you banished from there?

VALENTINE
I was.
I was.

Second Outlaw
For what offence?
For what crime?

VALENTINE
For that which now torments me to rehearse:
For one that now pains me to repeat:
I kill'd a man, whose death I much repent;
I killed a man, whose death I regret;
But yet I slew him manfully in fight,
But still I killed him bravely in a fight,
Without false vantage or base treachery.
Without an unfair advantage or dishonorable trickery.

First Outlaw
Why, ne'er repent it, if it were done so.
Well, don't regret it, if that's how it happened.
But were you banish'd for so small a fault?
But you were banished for such a small crime?

VALENTINE
I was, and held me glad of such a doom.
I was, and was glad to have such a sentence.

Second Outlaw
Have you the tongues?
Do you speak foreign languages?

VALENTINE
My youthful travel therein made me happy,
My youthful travel has made me accomplished with them,
Or else I often had been miserable.
Or else I would have often been unhappy.

Third Outlaw
By the bare scalp of Robin Hood's fat friar,
By the bald head of Robin Hood's fat friar,
This fellow were a king for our wild faction!
This fellow could be king of our wild group!

First Outlaw

We'll have him. Sirs, a word.
We'll have him. Men, let's talk.

SPEED

Master, be one of them; it's an honourable kind of thievery.
Master, become on of them; it's an honorable kind of robbery.

VALENTINE

Peace, villain!
Quiet, scoundrel!

Second Outlaw

Tell us this: have you any thing to take to?
Tell us this: do have any resources?

VALENTINE

Nothing but my fortune.
Nothing but my luck.

Third Outlaw

Know, then, that some of us are gentlemen,
Be aware, then, that some of us are gentlemen,
Such as the fury of ungovern'd youth
The kind that in the fury of reckless youth
Thrust from the company of awful men:
Were sent away from the company of respectful men:
Myself was from Verona banished
I was banished from Verona
For practising to steal away a lady,
For plotting to steal away a lady,
An heir, and near allied unto the duke.
An heiress, and closely related to the duke.

Second Outlaw

And I from Mantua, for a gentleman,
And I was banished from Mantua, because of a gentlemen
Who, in my mood, I stabb'd unto the heart.
Who I stabbed in the heart in anger.

First Outlaw

And I for such like petty crimes as these,

And I was too for little crimes like these,
But to the purpose--for we cite our faults,
But to the point—since we mention our crimes,
That they may hold excus'd our lawless lives;
So that they may justify our lives outside of the law;
And partly, seeing you are beautified
And in part, since we see that your are handsome
With goodly shape and by your own report
With a good figure and by your own claims
A linguist and a man of such perfection
A man of languages and such perfection
As we do in our quality much want—
Like we want in our companions—

Second Outlaw
Indeed, because you are a banish'd man,
Indeed, and because you have been banished,
Therefore, above the rest, we parley to you:
Because of that, above all other reasons, are we negotiating with you:
Are you content to be our general?
Are you willing to be our leader?
To make a virtue of necessity
To turn necessity into an advantage
And live, as we do, in this wilderness?
And live, like we do, in the wilderness?

Third Outlaw
What say'st thou? wilt thou be of our consort?
What do you say? Will you be part of our company?
Say ay, and be the captain of us all:
Say yes, and you'll be the leader of us all:
We'll do thee homage and be ruled by thee,
We'll pay our respects to you and be ruled by you,
Love thee as our commander and our king.
And love you as our commander and our king.

First Outlaw
But if thou scorn our courtesy, thou diest.
But if you reject our offer, you will die.

Second Outlaw
Thou shalt not live to brag what we have offer'd.
You will not live to brag about what we have offered you.

VALENTINE
I take your offer and will live with you,
I will take your offer and live with you,
Provided that you do no outrages
Provided that you don't harm
On silly women or poor passengers.
Helpless women or poor travelers.

Third Outlaw
No, we detest such vile base practises.
No, we hate such terrible, dishonorable practices.
Come, go with us, we'll bring thee to our crews,
Come on, come with us, and we'll bring you to our company,
And show thee all the treasure we have got,
And show you all the treasure we have gotten,
Which, with ourselves, all rest at thy dispose.
Which, along with ourselves, is all under your control.

Exeunt

SCENE II. Milan.

Outside the DUKE's palace, under SILVIA's chamber.

Enter PROTEUS

PROTEUS
Already have I been false to Valentine
Already I have been disloyal to Valentine
And now I must be as unjust to Thurio.
And now I must be unjust to Thurio.
Under the colour of commending him,
While pretending to speak well of him,
I have access my own love to prefer:
I have an opporunity to promote my own love instead:
But Silvia is too fair, too true, too holy,
But Silvia, is too beautiful, too honest, and too virtuous,
To be corrupted with my worthless gifts.
To be won over with my worthless gifts.
When I protest true loyalty to her,
When I swear true loyalty to her,
She twits me with my falsehood to my friend;
She criticizes me for my disloyalty to my friend;
When to her beauty I commend my vows,
When I declare my promises to her beauty,
She bids me think how I have been forsworn
She tells me to think of how I have broken my word
In breaking faith with Julia whom I loved:
By being disloyal to Julia whom I loved:
And notwithstanding all her sudden quips,
And in spite of all her biting insults,
The least whereof would quell a lover's hope,
The smallest of which would put out a lover's hope,
Yet, spaniel-like, the more she spurns my love,
Still, like a puppy, the more she rejects my love,
The more it grows and fawneth on her still.
The more my love grows and I continue to worship her.
But here comes Thurio: now must we to her window,
But here comes Thurio: now we must go to her window,
And give some evening music to her ear.
And play some evening music for her ear.

Enter THURIO and Musicians

THURIO
How now, Sir Proteus, are you crept before us?
What's this, Sir Proteus, have you sneakily gotten here before us?

PROTEUS
Ay, gentle Thurio: for you know that love
Yes, noble Thurio: because you know that love
Will creep in service where it cannot go.
Will sneak where it cannot openly walk.

THURIO
Ay, but I hope, sir, that you love not here.
Yes, but I hope, sir, that your love isn't here.

PROTEUS
Sir, but I do; or else I would be hence.
Sir, but it is; or else I wouldn't be here.

THURIO
Who? Silvia?
Who? Silvia?

PROTEUS
Ay, Silvia; for your sake.
Yes, Silvia; for you sake.

THURIO
I thank you for your own. Now, gentlemen,
Thank you for clarifying. Now, gentlemen,
Let's tune, and to it lustily awhile.
Let's play, and do it energetically for a while.

Enter, at a distance, Host, and JULIA in boy's clothes

Host
Now, my young guest, methinks you're allycholly: I
Now, my young guest, I seems to me that you're melancholy:
pray you, why is it?
Please, what is it?

JULIA

122

Marry, mine host, because I cannot be merry.
By Mary, my host, it's because I cannot be happy.

Host
Come, we'll have you merry: I'll bring you where
Come one, we'll make you happy: I'll bring you to where
you shall hear music and see the gentleman that you asked for.
You can hear music and see the gentlemen that you asked for.

JULIA
But shall I hear him speak?
But will I hear him speak?

Host
Ay, that you shall.
Yes, you will.

JULIA
That will be music.
That will be music to my ears.

Music plays

Host
Hark, hark!
Listen, listen!

JULIA
Is he among these?
Is he with them?

Host
Ay: but, peace! let's hear 'em.
Yes: but quiet! Let's listen to them.

SONG
Who is Silvia? what is she,
Who is Silvia? What is this woman
That all our swains commend her?
Who all these lover's praise?
Holy, fair and wise is she;
She is virtuous, beautiful and wise;
The heaven such grace did lend her,

The gods have her such elegance,
That she might admired be.
So that she would be admired.
Is she kind as she is fair?
Is she as kind as she is beautiful?
For beauty lives with kindness.
Because beauty lives with kindness.
Love doth to her eyes repair,
Love himself uses her eyes
To help him of his blindness,
To help him with his blindness,
And, being help'd, inhabits there.
And, being helped with it, he lives in there.
Then to Silvia let us sing,
So let us sing to Silvia,
That Silvia is excelling;
That Silvia is the best;
She excels each mortal thing
She surpasses each mortal creature
Upon the dull earth dwelling:
That lives on this dreary earth:
To her let us garlands bring.
Let us bring her garlands.

Host
How now! are you sadder than you were before? How
What's this! Are you more sad now than you were before? What's
do you, man? the music likes you not.
Wrong, man? You don't care for the music?

JULIA
You mistake; the musician likes me not.
You're mistaken; I don't care for the musician.

Host
Why, my pretty youth?
Why not, my pretty boy?

JULIA
He plays false, father.
He plays wrongly, father.

Host
How? out of tune on the strings?

How so? Are the strings out of tune?

JULIA

Not so; but yet so false that he grieves my very
No; but still it's so wrong that he upsets my very
heart-strings.
Heart-strings.

Host

You have a quick ear.
You have a sharp ear.

JULIA

Ay, I would I were deaf; it makes me have a slow heart.
Yes, but I wish I were deaf; my hearing makes me have a heavy heart.

Host

I perceive you delight not in music.
I see that you don't enjoy music.

JULIA

Not a whit, when it jars so.
Not at all, when it sounds so ugly.

Host

Hark, what fine change is in the music!
Listen, what nice variation there is in the music!

JULIA

Ay, that change is the spite.
Yes, that variation is what irritates me.

Host

You would have them always play but one thing?
You want them to always play the same thing?

JULIA

I would always have one play but one thing.
I want each one to play only one thing.
But, host, doth this Sir Proteus that we talk on
But, host, does this Sir Proteus that we've talked about
Often resort unto this gentlewoman?
Often visit this lady?

Host
I tell you what Launce, his man, told me: he loved
I'll tell you what Launce, his servant boy, told me: he loves
her out of all nick.
Her beyond measure.

JULIA
Where is Launce?
Where is Launce?

Host
Gone to seek his dog; which tomorrow, by his
He's gone to find his dog; which tomorrow, by his
master's command, he must carry for a present to his lady.
Master's command, he must bring as a present for this lady.

JULIA
Peace! stand aside: the company parts.
Quiet! Step aside: the company is leaving.

PROTEUS
Sir Thurio, fear not you: I will so plead
Sir Thurio, don't be afraid: I will speak for you so well
That you shall say my cunning drift excels.
That you will say my clever plan has worked.

THURIO
Where meet we?
Where will we meet?

PROTEUS
At Saint Gregory's well.
At the well of Saint Gregory.

THURIO
Farewell.
Goodbye.

Exeunt THURIO and Musicians

Enter SILVIA above

PROTEUS
Madam, good even to your ladyship.

Madam, good evening to you, my lady.

SILVIA
I thank you for your music, gentlemen.
Thank you for you music, gentlemen.
Who is that that spake?
Who is this speaking?

PROTEUS
One, lady, if you knew his pure heart's truth,
Someone, lady, who if you knew his heart's pure honesty,
You would quickly learn to know him by his voice.
You would quickly learn to recognize him by the sound of his voice.

SILVIA
Sir Proteus, as I take it.
It sounds like Sir Proteus.

PROTEUS
Sir Proteus, gentle lady, and your servant.
Sir Proteus, noble lady, who is your follower,

SILVIA
What's your will?
What do you want?

PROTEUS
That I may compass yours.
To win you over.

SILVIA
You have your wish; my will is even this:
You've done that; I want you to do this:
That presently you hie you home to bed.
Immediately hurry to your home and go to bed.
Thou subtle, perjured, false, disloyal man!
You tricky, lying, faithless, disloyal man!
Think'st thou I am so shallow, so conceitless,
Do you think that I am so shallow, so unintelligence,
To be seduced by thy flattery,
To be seduced by your flattery,
That hast deceived so many with thy vows?
When you have tricked so many other with your promises?
Return, return, and make thy love amends.

Return home, and make amends with your love , Julia.
For me, by this pale queen of night I swear,
As for me, I swear by the moon,
I am so far from granting thy request
That I am so far from being won over by you,
That I despise thee for thy wrongful suit,
And I hate you for dishonestly pursing me,
And by and by intend to chide myself
And soon I intend to scold myself
Even for this time I spend in talking to thee.
For even spending this much time talking to you.

PROTEUS
I grant, sweet love, that I did love a lady;
I admit, sweet love, that I did love another lady;
But she is dead.
But she is dead.

JULIA
[Aside] 'Twere false, if I should speak it;
[Aside] That's a lie, just as if I had said it;
For I am sure she is not buried.
For I know for sure that she isn't buried.

SILVIA
Say that she be; yet Valentine thy friend
Even if she is; your friend Valentine still
Survives; to whom, thyself art witness,
Lives; to whom, as you know yourself,
I am betroth'd: and art thou not ashamed
I intend to marry: and were you not ashamed
To wrong him with thy importunacy?
To betray him with your persistent pleas?

PROTEUS
I likewise hear that Valentine is dead.
I also hear that Valentine is dead.

SILVIA
And so suppose am I; for in his grave
And so I suppose that I am too; because in his grave,
Assure thyself my love is buried.
Rest assured, my love is already buried.

PROTEUS
Sweet lady, let me rake it from the earth.
Sweet lady, let me unbury it from the earth.

SILVIA
Go to thy lady's grave and call hers thence,
Got to your lady's grave and bring hers out,
Or, at the least, in hers sepulchre thine.
Or, at the very least, burry your love in her grave.

JULIA
[Aside] He heard not that.
[Aside] He didn't hear that.

PROTEUS
Madam, if your heart be so obdurate,
Madam, if your heart is so stubborn,
Vouchsafe me yet your picture for my love,
Allow me to have a picture of you for me to love,
The picture that is hanging in your chamber;
The picture that is hanging in your bedroom;
To that I'll speak, to that I'll sigh and weep:
I'll speak to it, I'll sigh and weep to it:
For since the substance of your perfect self
Because since your actual perfect self
Is else devoted, I am but a shadow;
Is devoted to someone else, I am only a shadow;
And to your shadow will I make true love.
And I will show my true love to your portrait.

JULIA
[Aside] If 'twere a substance, you would, sure, deceive it,
[Aside] If it were really her, you would, surely, be unfaithful to her,
And make it but a shadow, as I am.
And turn her into a ghost, as you did me.

SILVIA
I am very loath to be your idol, sir;
I am very reluctant to be the figure you worship, sir;
But since your falsehood shall become you well
But since it will be fitting for your dishonesty
To worship shadows and adore false shapes,
To worship portraits and adore artificial figures,
Send to me in the morning and I'll send it:

Send something to me in the mornings and I'll send it to you:
And so, good rest.
And now, good night.

PROTEUS
As wretches have o'ernight
I will wait overnight like criminal have
That wait for execution in the morn.
Who are waiting for their execution in the morning.

Exeunt PROTEUS and SILVIA severally

JULIA
Host, will you go?
Host, are you ready to go?

Host
By my halidom, I was fast asleep.
By all this is holy, I was fast asleep.

JULIA
Pray you, where lies Sir Proteus?
Please, tell me where Sir Proteus lives?

Host
Marry, at my house. Trust me, I think 'tis almost day.
By Mary, at my house. Believe me, I think it's almost daybreak.

JULIA
Not so; but it hath been the longest night
It's not; but it has been the longest night
That e'er I watch'd and the most heaviest.
That I have ever stayed awake for, and the most sad.

Exeunt

SCENE III. The same.

Enter EGLAMOUR

EGLAMOUR
This is the hour that Madam Silvia
This is the time that Madam Silvia
Entreated me to call and know her mind:
Asked me to visit and find out what she's thinking:
There's some great matter she'ld employ me in.
There's some great matter that she would like me to help with.
Madam, madam!
Madam, madam!

Enter SILVIA above

SILVIA
Who calls?
Who's calling?

EGLAMOUR
Your servant and your friend;
Your follower and your friend;
One that attends your ladyship's command.
Someone who waits for your command, my lady.

SILVIA
Sir Eglamour, a thousand times good morrow.
Sir Eglamour, a thousand times good morning.

EGLAMOUR
As many, worthy lady, to yourself:
And just as many to yourself, good lady:
According to your ladyship's impose,
According to your ladyship's command,
I am thus early come to know what service
I have come by this early to know what help
It is your pleasure to command me in.
You would like to have from me.

SILVIA

O Eglamour, thou art a gentleman—
Oh, Eglamour, you are a gentleman—
Think not I flatter, for I swear I do not—
Don't think I'm flattering you, because I swear I'm not—
Valiant, wise, remorseful, well accomplish'd:
You're brave, wise, caring, and very successful;
Thou art not ignorant what dear good will
You are aware what genuine love
I bear unto the banish'd Valentine,
I have for the exiled Valentine;
Nor how my father would enforce me marry
And how my father wants to force me to marry
Vain Thurio, whom my very soul abhors.
The foolish Thurio, who my very own soul hates.
Thyself hast loved; and I have heard thee say
You have been in love; and I have heard you say
No grief did ever come so near thy heart
That your heart never experience any grief
As when thy lady and thy true love died,
Like when your lady who was your true love died,
Upon whose grave thou vow'dst pure chastity.
And on whose grave you swore to never be with another woman.
Sir Eglamour, I would to Valentine,
Sir Eglamour, I want to go to Valentine,
To Mantua, where I hear he makes abode;
To Mantua, where I've heard he lives;
And, for the ways are dangerous to pass,
And, because the journey there is dangerous,
I do desire thy worthy company,
I would like your valuable company,
Upon whose faith and honour I repose.
Since I can happily rely on your faith and honor.
Urge not my father's anger, Eglamour,
Don't provoke my father's anger, Eglamour,
But think upon my grief, a lady's grief,
But think about my grief, a lady's grief,
And on the justice of my flying hence,
And about the righteousness of me escaping from here,
To keep me from a most unholy match,
To keep me away from a terrible marriage,
Which heaven and fortune still rewards with plagues.
Which heaven and luck always repay with misfortunes.
I do desire thee, even from a heart

I want you, even though my heart is
As full of sorrows as the sea of sands,
As full of sorrow as the sea is of sand,
To bear me company and go with me:
To keep me company and go with me:
If not, to hide what I have said to thee,
If not, I want you to keep secret what I have said to you,
That I may venture to depart alone.
So that I can try to leave on my own.

EGLAMOUR
Madam, I pity much your grievances;
Madam, I pity your distress;
Which since I know they virtuously are placed,
And since I know your requests are honorable,
I give consent to go along with you,
I agree to go with you,
Recking as little what betideth me
With as little care of what may happen to me
As much I wish all good befortune you.
As I greatly wish that only good happens to you.
When will you go?
When would you like to go?

SILVIA
This evening coming.
This coming evening.

EGLAMOUR
Where shall I meet you?
Where should I meet you?

SILVIA
At Friar Patrick's cell,
At Friar Patrick's room,
Where I intend holy confession.
Where I make my holy confessions.

EGLAMOUR
I will not fail your ladyship. Good morrow, gentle lady.
I will not fail you, my lady. Good morning, noble lady.

SILVIA
Good morrow, kind Sir Eglamour.

Good morning, kind Sir Eglamour.

Exeunt severally

SCENE IV. The same.

Enter LAUNCE, with his Dog

LAUNCE
When a man's servant shall play the cur with him,
When a man's dog makes him seem like a dog,
look you, it goes hard: one that I brought up of a
It's a hard thing, I tell you: I brought him up from a
puppy; one that I saved from drowning, when three or
Puppy; I saved him from drowning, when three or
four of his blind brothers and sisters went to it.
Four of his still blind brothers and sisters were drowned.
I have taught him, even as one would say precisely,
I have taught him, exactly as one would say,
'thus I would teach a dog.' I was sent to deliver
'This is how I would teach a dog.' I was sent to deliver
him as a present to Mistress Silvia from my master;
him as a present to Mistress Silvia from my master;
and I came no sooner into the dining-chamber but he
And no sooner then I have come into the dining room, he
steps me to her trencher and steals her capon's leg:
Walks us over to her plate and steals her chicken leg:
O, 'tis a foul thing when a cur cannot keep himself
Oh, it's a terrible thing when a dog can't control himself
in all companies! I would have, as one should say,
In anyone's company! I have, as they say,
one that takes upon him to be a dog indeed, to be,
A dog that takes it upon himself to really be dog, to be
as it were, a dog at all things. If I had not had
Really experienced at being a dog, as it were. If I didn't have
more wit than he, to take a fault upon me that he did,
More intelligence than he does, so that I took the blame on myself for what he did,
I think verily he had been hanged for't; sure as I
I think he would really have been killed for it; as surely as I
live, he had suffered for't; you shall judge. He
Live, he would have suffered for it; you can be the judge of that. He
thrusts me himself into the company of three or four
Shoved himself into the company of three of four
gentlemanlike dogs under the duke's table: he had

Noble dogs under the duke's table: he had
not been there--bless the mark!--a pissing while, but
Only been there—pardon the phrase!—the short time it takes to piss, before
all the chamber smelt him. 'Out with the dog!' says
The whole room could smell him 'Get that dog out!' said
one: 'What cur is that?' says another: 'Whip him
One person: 'What mutt is that?' said another: 'Whip him
out' says the third: 'Hang him up' says the duke.
Out of here' said a third: 'Have him killed' says the duke.
I, having been acquainted with the smell before,
I, since I had smelled that smell before,
knew it was Crab, and goes me to the fellow that
Knew that it was Crab, and I went to the man that
whips the dogs: 'Friend,' quoth I, 'you mean to whip
Whips the dogs: 'Friend,' I said, 'do you intend to whip
the dog?' 'Ay, marry, do I,' quoth he. 'You do him
This dog?' 'Yes, by Mary, I do,' he said. 'You would be whipping him
the more wrong,' quoth I; ''twas I did the thing you
Mistakenly,' I said; 'it was me that did the thing you
wot of.' He makes me no more ado, but whips me out
Were told of.' He took no more time, but whipped me out
of the chamber. How many masters would do this for
Of the chamber. How many master would do this for
his servant? Nay, I'll be sworn, I have sat in the
His dog? No, I swear, I have sat in the
stocks for puddings he hath stolen, otherwise he had
Chains for sausages he stole, because otherwise he would have
been executed; I have stood on the pillory for geese
Been killed; I have stood locked up for geese
he hath killed, otherwise he had suffered for't.
He killed, because otherwise he would have suffered for it.
Thou thinkest not of this now. Nay, I remember the
Don't think about it now. No, I remember the
trick you served me when I took my leave of Madam
Trick you, Crab, played on me when I took you to Madam
Silvia: did not I bid thee still mark me and do as I
Silvia; didn't I ask you to pay attention to me and do as I
do? when didst thou see me heave up my leg and make
Do? When did you ever see me lift up my leg and
water against a gentlewoman's farthingale? Didst
Pee on a lady's hooped petticoat? Did
thou ever see me do such a trick?
You ever see me do such a trick?

Enter PROTEUS and JULIA

PROTEUS
Sebastian is thy name? I like thee well
Sebastian is you name? I like you
And will employ thee in some service presently.
And will hire you to do something for my right now.

JULIA
In what you please: I'll do what I can.
Whatever you like: I'll do what I can.

PROTEUS
I hope thou wilt.
I hope you will.

To LAUNCE

How now, you whoreson peasant!
What no, you peasant son of a whore!
Where have you been these two days loitering?
Where have you been lurking the past two days?

LAUNCE
Marry, sir, I carried Mistress Silvia the dog you bade me.
By Mary, sir, I brought Mistress Silvia the dog that you asked me to.

PROTEUS
And what says she to my little jewel?
And what did she say to my little gift?

LAUNCE
Marry, she says your dog was a cur, and tells you
By Mary, she said that the dog was a matt, and to tell you
currish thanks is good enough for such a present.
Mean-spirited thanks is good enough for such a present.

PROTEUS
But she received my dog?
But she kept my dog?

LAUNCE
No, indeed, did she not: here have I brought him

No, indeed, she didn't: I have brought him
back again.
Back here again.

PROTEUS
What, didst thou offer her this from me?
What, didn't you offer her this gift from me?

LAUNCE
Ay, sir: the other squirrel was stolen from me by
Yeah, sir: because the other small dog was stolen from me by
the hangman boys in the market-place: and then I
The devilish boys in the market-place: and then I
offered her mine own, who is a dog as big as ten of
Offered her my own dog, who is bigger than ten of
yours, and therefore the gift the greater.
Your dogs, and so he is a better gift.

PROTEUS
Go get thee hence, and find my dog again,
Go get out of here, and find my little dog again,
Or ne'er return again into my sight.
Or never come back to my sight.
Away, I say! stay'st thou to vex me here?
Get away, I say! Do you just stay to anger me?

Exit LAUNCE

A slave, that still an end turns me to shame!
A servant, who always humiliates me!
Sebastian, I have entertained thee,
Sebastian, I have hired you,
Partly that I have need of such a youth
Partly because I need such a young man
That can with some discretion do my business,
That can do my business with some tact,
For 'tis no trusting to yond foolish lout,
Because I can't trust that foolish lout over there,
But chiefly for thy face and thy behavior,
But mainly because of your face and your behavior,
Which, if my augury deceive me not,
Which, if my good judgment doesn't deceive me,
Witness good bringing up, fortune and truth:

Show that you have had a good upbringing, had good fortune and are honest:
Therefore know thou, for this I entertain thee.
So be aware, that this is why I hired you.
Go presently and take this ring with thee,
Go immediately and take his ring with you,
Deliver it to Madam Silvia:
And deliver it to Madam Silvia:
She loved me well deliver'd it to me.
The woman who gave this to me loved me a lot.

JULIA
It seems you loved not her, to leave her token.
It seems like you didn't love her, to give up her love-token.
She is dead, belike?
Is she dead, perhaps?

PROTEUS
Not so; I think she lives.
No she's not; I think she's alive.

JULIA
Alas!
Sadly!

PROTEUS
Why dost thou cry 'alas'?
Why did you just cry out 'sadly'?

JULIA
I cannot choose
I cannot help
But pity her.
But feel sorry for her.

PROTEUS
Wherefore shouldst thou pity her?
Why should you feel sorry for her?

JULIA
Because methinks that she loved you as well
Because it seems to me that she loved you as much
As you do love your lady Silvia:
As you love your lady Silvia:
She dreams of him that has forgot her love;

She dream of the man who was forgotten her love;
You dote on her that cares not for your love.
And you worship a woman that doesn't care for your lov;
'Tis pity love should be so contrary;
It's a shame that love is so uncooperative;
And thinking of it makes me cry 'alas!'
And thinking of that made me cry out 'sadly!'

PROTEUS

Well, give her that ring and therewithal
Well, give her that ring and with it
This letter. That's her chamber. Tell my lady
This letter. That' her room there. Tell my lady
I claim the promise for her heavenly picture.
That I'm claiming the promise of her heavenly picture.
Your message done, hie home unto my chamber,
When you message is done, hurry home to my room,
Where thou shalt find me, sad and solitary.
Where you sill find me, sad and alone.

Exit

JULIA

How many women would do such a message?
How many women could deliver such a message?
Alas, poor Proteus! thou hast entertain'd
It's a shame, poor Proteus! You have hired
A fox to be the shepherd of thy lambs.
A fox to be the shepherd of your lambs.
Alas, poor fool! why do I pity him
It's a shame, poor fool! Why do I feel sorry for him
That with his very heart despiseth me?
Who hates me with his heart?
Because he loves her, he despiseth me;
Because he loves her, he hates me;
Because I love him I must pity him.
Because I love him, I must feel sorry for him.
This ring I gave him when he parted from me,
This is the ring that I gave him when he left me,
To bind him to remember my good will;
To make him remember my love;
And now am I, unhappy messenger,
And now I am, unhappy messenger that I am,
To plead for that which I would not obtain,

Supposed to plead for the love of Silvia for Proteus, which I don't want to obtain,
To carry that which I would have refused,
To carry the ring and letter that I would have refused,
To praise his faith which I would have dispraised.
To praise his loyalty, which I want to criticize.
I am my master's true-confirmed love;
I am my master's true love;
But cannot be true servant to my master,
But I cannot be an honest servant to my master,
Unless I prove false traitor to myself.
Unless I act as a traitor to myself.
Yet will I woo for him, but yet so coldly
But I will woo her for him, but still so hardheartedly,
As, heaven it knows, I would not have him speed.
Since, as heaven knows, I don't want him to succeed.

Enter SILVIA, attended

Gentlewoman, good day! I pray you, be my mean
My Lady, good day! Please, would you
To bring me where to speak with Madam Silvia.
Bring me to where I can speak with Madam Silvia.

SILVIA
What would you with her, if that I be she?
What would you say to her, if I was her?

JULIA
If you be she, I do entreat your patience
If you are her, I ask for you patience
To hear me speak the message I am sent on.
To listen to me tell you the message I was sent to give.

SILVIA
From whom?
From whom?

JULIA
From my master, Sir Proteus, madam.
From my master, Sir Proteus, madam.

SILVIA
O, he sends you for a picture.
Oh, he sent you to get the picture.

JULIA
Ay, madam.
Yes, madam.

SILVIA
Ursula, bring my picture here.
Ursula, bring my picture here/
Go give your master this: tell him from me,
Go and give your master this: give him this message from me:
One Julia, that his changing thoughts forget,
The woman Julia, that he has forgotten since he changed his mind,
Would better fit his chamber than this shadow.
Would be more suitable for his bedroom than this portrait.

JULIA
Madam, please you peruse this letter.—
Madam, please read this letter—
Pardon me, madam; I have unadvised
Forgive me, madaml I have accidently
Deliver'd you a paper that I should not:
Given you a letter that I shouldn't have:

"[JULIA take back the first letter and gives SILVIA a different letter than before.]"

This is the letter to your ladyship.
This here is the letter to you, your lady.

SILVIA
I pray thee, let me look on that again.
Please, let me look at that one again.

JULIA
It may not be; good madam, pardon me.
I can't; good madam, forgive me.

SILVIA
There, hold!
Wait there!

"[SILVIA tear apart the letter]"

I will not look upon your master's lines:

I won't read whatever your master wrote:
I know they are stuff'd with protestations
I know it's jam-packed with declarations
And full of new-found oaths; which he will break
And full of newly created promises; which he will break
As easily as I do tear his paper.
As easily as I tore that paper.

JULIA
Madam, he sends your ladyship this ring.
Madam, he sends you this wring, your lady.

SILVIA
The more shame for him that he sends it me;
And more shame on him who send it to me;
For I have heard him say a thousand times
Because I have heard him say a thousand times
His Julia gave it him at his departure.
That Julia gave it to him at his departure.
Though his false finger have profaned the ring,
Though his unfaithful finger has already abused the ring,
Mine shall not do his Julia so much wrong.
My finger will not do his Julia any harm.

JULIA
She thanks you.
She thanks you.

SILVIA
What say'st thou?
What did you say?

JULIA
I thank you, madam, that you tender her.
I thank you, madam, that you are concerned for her.
Poor gentlewoman! my master wrongs her much.
Poor lady! My master mistreats her so much.

SILVIA
Dost thou know her?
Do you know her?

JULIA
Almost as well as I do know myself:

Almost as well as I know myself:
To think upon her woes I do protest
I'll tell you that thinking about her troubles,
That I have wept a hundred several times.
I have cried several hundred times.

SILVIA
Belike she thinks that Proteus hath forsook her.
It seems to me that she think that Proteus has rejected her.

JULIA
I think she doth; and that's her cause of sorrow.
I think she does; and that's the cause of her sorrow.

SILVIA
Is she not passing fair?
Is she not extremely pretty?

JULIA
She hath been fairer, madam, than she is:
She has been prettier, madam, than she is now:
When she did think my master loved her well,
When she thought my master still loved her,
She, in my judgment, was as fair as you:
She was a pretty as you, by my judgment:
But since she did neglect her looking-glass
But since then she stopped looking in the mirror
And threw her sun-expelling mask away,
And threw away the mask that protects her skin from the sun,
The air hath starved the roses in her cheeks
The air has wither the rosiness of her cheeks
And pinch'd the lily-tincture of her face,
And worn away the pale complexion of her face,
That now she is become as black as I.
That now she is as ugly as I am.

SILVIA
How tall was she?
How tall was she?

JULIA
About my stature; for at Pentecost,
About my height; because on Pentecost,
When all our pageants of delight were play'd,

When we put on all your pageant plays,
Our youth got me to play the woman's part,
Our young man got me to play a woman's part,
And I was trimm'd in Madam Julia's gown,
And I was dressed in Madam Julia's gown,
Which served me as fit, by all men's judgments,
Which fit me just as well, by everyone's judgements,
As if the garment had been made for me:
As if the dress had been made for me:
Therefore I know she is about my height.
That's how I know she is about my height.
And at that time I made her weep agood,
And at the time I made her weep in earnest,
For I did play a lamentable part:
Because I played a mournful part:
Madam, 'twas Ariadne passioning
Madam, it was Ariadne in a passion and grieving
For Theseus' perjury and unjust flight;
For Theseus' dishonesty and deceitful escape;
Which I so lively acted with my tears
Which I aced out so energetically with my tears
That my poor mistress, moved therewithal,
That my poor mistress, moved by the performance,
Wept bitterly; and would I might be dead
Wept bitterly; and I'd wish I were dead
If I in thought felt not her very sorrow!
If I had not felt her same exact sorrow in my own mind!

SILVIA
She is beholding to thee, gentle youth.
She is indebted to you, kind young man.
Alas, poor lady, desolate and left!
It's a same, poor lady, deserted and alone!
I weep myself to think upon thy words.
I myself am weeping to think about your words.
Here, youth, there is my purse; I give thee this
Here, young man, this is my purse; I'm giving it to you
For thy sweet mistress' sake, because thou lovest her.
For you sweet mistress' sake, because you love her.
Farewell.
Goodbye.

Exit SILVIA, with attendants

JULIA

And she shall thank you for't, if e'er you know her.
And she will thank you for it, if you ever meet her.
A virtuous gentlewoman, mild and beautiful!
A virtuous lady, kind and beautiful!
I hope my master's suit will be but cold,
I hope my master's pursuit of her won't work,
Since she respects my mistress' love so much.
Since she respects my mistress Julia's love so much.
Alas, how love can trifle with itself!
It's a shame, how love can mess with itself!
Here is her picture: let me see; I think,
Here is her picture: let me see, I think,
If I had such a tire, this face of mine
If I had such a tiara, my face
Were full as lovely as is this of hers:
Would be just as pretty as hers is:
And yet the painter flatter'd her a little,
And still the painter painted her a bit prettier than she is,
Unless I flatter with myself too much.
Unless I'm just flattering myself too much.
Her hair is auburn, mine is perfect yellow:
Her hair is auburn, and mine is golden blonde:
If that be all the difference in his love,
If that is the only difference in his love,
I'll get me such a colour'd periwig.
I can get myself a wig of that color.
Her eyes are grey as glass, and so are mine:
Her eyes are bluish grey, and so are mine;
Ay, but her forehead's low, and mine's as high.
Yes, but her forehead is a bit low, and mine is high.
What should it be that he respects in her
What is it that he values in her
But I can make respective in myself,
That I can't inspire the same in myself.
If this fond Love were not a blinded god?
What if passionate love were not a blind god?
Come, shadow, come and take this shadow up,
Come on, ghost of Julia, pick this portrait up,
For 'tis thy rival. O thou senseless form,
For it is your rival. Oh, you picture without human feeling,
Thou shalt be worshipp'd, kiss'd, loved and adored!
You will be worhshipped, kissed, loved and adored!
And, were there sense in his idolatry,

And, if his worship made any sense,
My substance should be statue in thy stead.
My actual self would be worship in its place.
I'll use thee kindly for thy mistress' sake,
I'll treat you well for your mistress' sake,
That used me so; or else, by Jove I vow,
Who treated me kindly; or otherwise, I swear by Jove,
I should have scratch'd out your unseeing eyes
I would have scratched out your unseeing eyes
To make my master out of love with thee!
To make my master fall out of love with you!

Exit

ACT V

SCENE I. Milan.

An abbey.

Enter EGLAMOUR

EGLAMOUR
The sun begins to gild the western sky;
The sunset it turning the sky gold,
And now it is about the very hour
And this is the time
That Silvia, at Friar Patrick's cell, should meet me.
That Silvia is meeting me in Friar Patrick's room.
She will not fail, for lovers break not hours,
She's won't fail, because lovers don't miss their appointments,
Unless it be to come before their time;
Unless it is to because they arrive early;
So much they spur their expedition.
So that they hurry up their speed.
See where she comes.
See here she comes.

Enter SILVIA

Lady, a happy evening!
Lady, good evening!

SILVIA
Amen, amen! Go on, good Eglamour,
So it is, so it is! Come on, good Eglamour,
Out at the postern by the abbey-wall:
Let's go out by the side gate by the abbey wall:
I fear I am attended by some spies.
I'm afraid that I'm followed by spies.

EGLAMOUR
Fear not: the forest is not three leagues off;
Don't be afraid: the forest is less than nine miles away;
If we recover that, we are sure enough.
If we reach there, we are safe enough.

Exeunt

SCENE II. The same.

The DUKE's palace.

Enter THURIO, PROTEUS, and JULIA

THURIO
Sir Proteus, what says Silvia to my suit?
Sir Proteus, what did Silvia say to my romantic pursuit?

PROTEUS
O, sir, I find her milder than she was;
Oh, sir, I found her to be more gentle than she usually is;
And yet she takes exceptions at your person.
But still she dislikes your appearance.

THURIO
What, that my leg is too long?
What, does she think my legs are too long?

PROTEUS
No; that it is too little.
No; that they are too skinny.

THURIO
I'll wear a boot, to make it somewhat rounder.
I'll wear boots, to make them seem bigger.

JULIA
[Aside] But love will not be spurr'd to what it loathes.
[Aside] But love will not be encouraged to love what it hates.

THURIO
What says she to my face?
What does she say about my face?

PROTEUS
She says it is a fair one.
She says it is pale.

THURIO

Nay then, the wanton lies; my face is black.
No then, the stubborn woman lies; my face is dark.

PROTEUS

But pearls are fair; and the old saying is,
But pearls are pale; and the old saying says,
Black men are pearls in beauteous ladies' eyes.
Dark men are pearls in beautiful ladies' eyes.

JULIA

[Aside] 'Tis true; such pearls as put out ladies' eyes;
[Aside] It's true; the kind of pearls that block out ladies' eyes like cataracts;
For I had rather wink than look on them.
Because I would rather close my eyes than look at them.

THURIO

How likes she my discourse?
How did she like my words?

PROTEUS

Ill, when you talk of war.
Not well, when you're talking about war.

THURIO

But well, when I discourse of love and peace?
Well then, what about when I talk about love and peace?

JULIA

[Aside] But better, indeed, when you hold your peace.
[Aside] The best, indeed, is when you are silent.

THURIO

What says she to my valour?
What does she say about my honor?

PROTEUS

O, sir, she makes no doubt of that.
Oh, sir, she doesn't question that.

JULIA

[Aside] She needs not, when she knows it cowardice.
[Aside] She doesn't need to, since she knows it is fear.

THURIO

What says she to my birth?
What does she say about my lineage?

PROTEUS
That you are well derived.
That you have come from a good family.

JULIA
[Aside] True; from a gentleman to a fool.
[Aside] It's true; you went from a gentlemen to a fool.

THURIO
Considers she my possessions?
Does she think about my belongings?

PROTEUS
O, ay; and pities them.
Oh, yes; and feels sorry for them.

THURIO
Wherefore?
Why?

JULIA
[Aside] That such an ass should owe them.
[Aside] Because such an ass owns them.

PROTEUS
That they are out by lease.
Because they are borrowed from others.

JULIA
Here comes the duke.
Here comes the duke.

Enter DUKE

DUKE
How now, Sir Proteus! how now, Thurio!
How are you, Sir Proteus! How are you, Thurio!
Which of you saw Sir Eglamour of late?
Have either of you send Sir Eglamour lately?

THURIO

Not I.
I haven't.

PROTEUS
Nor I.
Neither have I.

DUKE
Saw you my daughter?
Have you seen my daughter?

PROTEUS
Neither.
I haven't seen her either.

DUKE
Why then,
Well then,
She's fled unto that peasant Valentine;
She has run away to that scoundrel Valentine;
And Eglamour is in her company.
And Eglamour is with her.
'Tis true; for Friar Laurence met them both,
It's true, because Friar Laurence saw them both,
As he in penance wander'd through the forest;
While he was wandering though the forest doing his ritual apologies.
Him he knew well, and guess'd that it was she,
He recognizes Eglamour, and guessed that it was Silvia,
But, being mask'd, he was not sure of it;
Though, since she had a mask on, he wasn't sure;
Besides, she did intend confession
Besides, she was going to do her holy confession
At Patrick's cell this even; and there she was not;
In Friar Patrick's room this evening; and she wasn't there;
These likelihoods confirm her flight from hence.
These circumstances prove that she has run away from here.
Therefore, I pray you, stand not to discourse,
So, please, don't waste time talking,
But mount you presently and meet with me
But get your horses immediately and meet me
Upon the rising of the mountain-foot
At the beginning of the hills
That leads towards Mantua, whither they are fled:

That lead towards Mantua, where they are headed:
Dispatch, sweet gentlemen, and follow me.
Hurry up, good gentlemen, and follow me.

Exit

THURIO
Why, this it is to be a peevish girl,
Why, this is what it means to be a stubborn girl,
That flies her fortune when it follows her.
Who runs away from her good fortune when it pursues her, as I have for her hand in marriage.
I'll after, more to be revenged on Eglamour
I'll follow, more so that I can take revenge on Eglamour
Than for the love of reckless Silvia.
Than because I love the reckless Silvia.

Exit

PROTEUS
And I will follow, more for Silvia's love
And I will follow, more because I love Silvia
Than hate of Eglamour that goes with her.
Than because I hate Eglamour who is with her.

Exit

JULIA
And I will follow, more to cross that love
And I will follow, more so that I can prevent that love
Than hate for Silvia that is gone for love.
Than because of hatred towards Silvia who has run away for love.

Exit

SCENE III. The frontiers of Mantua.

The forest.

Enter Outlaws with SILVIA

First Outlaw
Come, come,
Come on, come on,
Be patient; we must bring you to our captain.
Be patient; we must bring you to our leader.

SILVIA
A thousand more mischances than this one
A thousand other misfortunes besides this one
Have learn'd me how to brook this patiently.
Have taught me how to tolerate this patiently.

Second Outlaw
Come, bring her away.
Come on, take her away.

First Outlaw
Where is the gentleman that was with her?
Where is the gentleman that was with her?

Third Outlaw
Being nimble-footed, he hath outrun us,
Since he was quick, he escaped us.
But Moyses and Valerius follow him.
But Moyses and Valerius are following him.
Go thou with her to the west end of the wood;
Take her with you to the west side of the forest;
There is our captain: we'll follow him that's fled;
Our leader is there: we'll follow the man who ran away;
The thicket is beset; he cannot 'scape.
The forest is surrounded; he cannot escape.

First Outlaw
Come, I must bring you to our captain's cave:

Come one, I must take you to your leader's cave:
Fear not; he bears an honourable mind,
Don't be afraid; he is an honorable character,
And will not use a woman lawlessly.
And will not handle a woman against the law.

SILVIA
O Valentine, this I endure for thee!
Oh, Valentine, I suffer this for you!

Exeunt

SCENE IV. Another part of the forest.

Enter VALENTINE

VALENTINE
How use doth breed a habit in a man!
How habits become routine for a man!
This shadowy desert, unfrequented woods,
This shadowy wilderness, secluded woods,
I better brook than flourishing peopled towns:
I am tolerating better than prosperous towns full of people:
Here can I sit alone, unseen of any,
Here I can sit alone, without anyone seeing me,
And to the nightingale's complaining notes
And to the sound of the nightingale's sad song
Tune my distresses and record my woes.
I can sing my misfortune and sound out my sadness.
O thou that dost inhabit in my breast,
Oh, Love, you who live in my heart,
Leave not the mansion so long tenantless,
Don't leave that place uninhabited for so long,
Lest, growing ruinous, the building fall
In case the structure of my heart might fall as it decays
And leave no memory of what it was!
And no one will remember it!
Repair me with thy presence, Silvia;
Revive me with your presence, Silvia;
Thou gentle nymph, cherish thy forlorn swain!
You gentle little goddess, cherish your abandoned lover!
What halloing and what stir is this to-day?
What's this shouting and what's this disruption right now?
These are my mates, that make their wills their law,
Those are my companions, who make their rules based on their own desires,
Have some unhappy passenger in chase.
And who are chasing some unlucky traveler.
They love me well; yet I have much to do
They love me well; but it takes a lot of work
To keep them from uncivil outrages.
To keep them from committing barbarian like outrages.
Withdraw thee, Valentine: who's this comes here?
Step away, Valentine: who's that coming here?

Enter PROTEUS, SILVIA, and JULIA

PROTEUS
Madam, this service I have done for you,
Madam, I have done this service for you,
Though you respect not aught your servant doth,
Although you don't respect anything that I do for you,
To hazard life and rescue you from him
To rise my life and rescue you from the man
That would have forced your honour and your love;
Who would have forced you to lose your honor and your virginity;
Vouchsafe me, for my meed, but one fair look;
Give me, as a reward, just one favorable glance;
A smaller boon than this I cannot beg
I cannot ask a smaller request than this,
And less than this, I am sure, you cannot give.
And, I'm sure, You couldn't give anything less.

VALENTINE
[Aside] How like a dream is this I see and hear!
[Aside] What I'm seeing and hearing is so much like a dream!
Love, lend me patience to forbear awhile.
Love, give me patience to control myself for a while.

SILVIA
O miserable, unhappy that I am!
Oh I am miserable and unhappy!

PROTEUS
Unhappy were you, madam, ere I came;
You were unhappy, madam, before I came;
But by my coming I have made you happy.
But I have made you happy by coming here.

SILVIA
By thy approach thou makest me most unhappy.
Your romantic advances make me more unhappy than anything else.

JULIA
[Aside] And me, when he approacheth to your presence.
[Aside] Me too, when the romantic advances are towards you.

SILVIA

Had I been seized by a hungry lion,
I wish I had been grabbed by hungry lion,
I would have been a breakfast to the beast,
I wish I would have been breakfast for the beast,
Rather than have false Proteus rescue me.
Instead of having the faithless Proteus rescue me.
O, Heaven be judge how I love Valentine,
Oh, Heaven knows how I love Valentine,
Whose life's as tender to me as my soul!
Whose life is as previous to me as my own soul!
And full as much, for more there cannot be,
And just as much, for there cannot be more,
I do detest false perjured Proteus.
I hate the dishonest liar Proteus.
Therefore be gone; solicit me no more.
So go away; don't pursue me any more.

PROTEUS
What dangerous action, stood it next to death,
There's no dangerous feat, even if it was close to death,
Would I not undergo for one calm look!
That I wouldn't go through for just one serene look!
O, 'tis the curse in love, and still approved,
Oh, it's the curse of love, and constantly proved,
When women cannot love where they're beloved!
That women cannot love the one who loves them.

SILVIA
When Proteus cannot love where he's beloved.
And that Proteus cannot love the one who loves him.
Read over Julia's heart, thy first best love,
Remember Julia's love, your first and better love,
For whose dear sake thou didst then rend thy faith
For whose dear sake you split your faithfulness apart
Into a thousand oaths; and all those oaths
Into a thousand promises; and all those promises
Descended into perjury, to love me.
Became lives so that you could love me.
Thou hast no faith left now, unless thou'dst two;
You have no faithfulness left now, unless you had two;
And that's far worse than none; better have none
And that's much worse than having none; it would be better to have no faithfulness
Than plural faith which is too much by one:

Than to be able to be faithful to more than one woman:
Thou counterfeit to thy true friend!
You are a fake comrade to your true friend!

PROTEUS
In love
When you're in love
Who respects friend?
Who think about their friends?

SILVIA
All men but Proteus.
Every man except Proteus.

PROTEUS
Nay, if the gentle spirit of moving words
No, if the peaceful nature of emotional words
Can no way change you to a milder form,
Can't change you at all to behave more gently,
I'll woo you like a soldier, at arms' end,
Then I'll win you over like a soldier, at sword point,
And love you 'gainst the nature of love,--force ye.
And love you opposite to the way love is naturally—I'll force you.

SILVIA
O heaven!
Oh heaven!

PROTEUS
I'll force thee yield to my desire.
I'll force you to give in to my desire.

VALENTINE
Ruffian, let go that rude uncivil touch,
Scoundrel, let go with that brutish, uncivilized hand,
Thou friend of an ill fashion!
You are an evil kind of friend!

PROTEUS
Valentine!
Valentine!

VALENTINE
Thou common friend, that's without faith or love,

You ordinary friend, who is without loyalty or love,
For such is a friend now; treacherous man!
Because that's what a friend is now; you disloyal man!
Thou hast beguiled my hopes; nought but mine eye
You have cheated my hopes; nothing but my own eyes
Could have persuaded me: now I dare not say
Could have convinced me that it was you: but now I can't say if
I have one friend alive; thou wouldst disprove me.
I have even one friend alive; you would prove me wrong.
Who should be trusted, when one's own right hand
Who can be trusted, when one's own best friend
Is perjured to the bosom? Proteus,
Is a liar to the core? Proteus
I am sorry I must never trust thee more,
I am sorry that I can never trust you again,
But count the world a stranger for thy sake.
But instead consider everyone a stranger because of you.
The private wound is deepest: O time most accurst,
The most personal injury is the most painful: Oh cursed time,
'Mongst all foes that a friend should be the worst!
Out of all enemies, a friend is the worse one!

PROTEUS
My shame and guilt confounds me.
I am overcome by my shame and guilt.
Forgive me, Valentine: if hearty sorrow
Forgive me, Valentine: if heartfelt remorse
Be a sufficient ransom for offence,
Is an adequate repayment for such a betray,
I tender 't here; I do as truly suffer
I am offering it to you now; I am suffering as honestly
As e'er I did commit.
As I ever did anything wrong.

VALENTINE
Then I am paid;
Then I am repaid;
And once again I do receive thee honest.
And once again I consider you to be honest.
Who by repentance is not satisfied
Whoever is not satisfied by remorse
Is nor of heaven nor earth, for these are pleased.
Is not from heaven or earth, since men from these places can be please;
By penitence the Eternal's wrath's appeased:

God's wrath is satisfied with atonement:
And, that my love may appear plain and free,
And, so that I can prove my friendship is given honestly and freely,
All that was mine in Silvia I give thee.
The hand that Silvia was going to give to me in marriage is now yours

JULIA
O me unhappy!
Oh, so much misfortune for me!

Swoons

"[JULIA faints]"

PROTEUS
Look to the boy.
Look at the boy.

VALENTINE
Why, boy! why, wag! how now! what's the matter?
Why, boy! Why did you faint, lad! What happened! What's the matter?
Look up; speak.
Look up at me; tell me what's wrong.

JULIA
O good sir, my master charged me to deliver a ring
Oh good sir, my master ordered me to deliver a ring
to Madam Silvia, which, out of my neglect, was never done.
To Madam Silvia, which I never did because I forgot.

PROTEUS
Where is that ring, boy?
Where is that ring, boy?

JULIA
Here 'tis; this is it.
It's right here; this is it.

"[JULIA hands him her own ring]"

PROTEUS
How! let me see:
What! Let me see it:
Why, this is the ring I gave to Julia.

Why, this sit he ring that I gave to Julia.

JULIA
O, cry you mercy, sir, I have mistook:
Oh, forgive me, sir, I was mistaken:
This is the ring you sent to Silvia.
This is the ring you sent to Silvia.

"[JULIA hands him the other ring]"

PROTEUS
But how camest thou by this ring? At my depart
But how did you get this ring? When I left
I gave this unto Julia.
I gave this to Julia.

JULIA
And Julia herself did give it me;
And Julia herself have it to me;
And Julia herself hath brought it hither.
And Julia herself sent me here.

PROTEUS
How! Julia!
What's this! Julia!

JULIA
Behold her that gave aim to all thy oaths,
Look on the woman who was the target of all your promises,
And entertain'd 'em deeply in her heart.
And who held them deeply in her heart.
How oft hast thou with perjury cleft the root!
How often you have split the bottom of my heart with your lies!
O Proteus, let this habit make thee blush!
Oh, Proteus, I hope my disguise makes you blush!
Be thou ashamed that I have took upon me
Be ashamed that I took upon myself
Such an immodest raiment, if shame live
Such inappropriate clothing for a woman, if it is in fact shameful
In a disguise of love:
To take on a disguise for the sake of love:
It is the lesser blot, modesty finds,
According to good manners, there is less shame
Women to change their shapes than men their minds.

For a woman to change her appearance that for a man to change his mind.

PROTEUS
Than men their minds! 'tis true.
For a man to change his mind! It's true.
O heaven! were man
Oh, heaven! If man were
But constant, he were perfect. That one error
Only faithful, he would be perfect. The one mistake
Fills him with faults; makes him run through all the sins:
Fills him with bad traits; and makes him commit all the sins:
Inconstancy falls off ere it begins.
Disloyalty ends before it begins.
What is in Silvia's face, but I may spy
What do I see in Silvia's face, that I don't find
More fresh in Julia's with a constant eye?
More beautiful in Julia's when my eyes are faithful?

VALENTINE
Come, come, a hand from either:
Come here, come here, each of you give me your hand:
Let me be blest to make this happy close;
Let me bless this happy union;
'Twere pity two such friends should be long foes.
It was such a shame that two such lover were enemies for so long.

PROTEUS
Bear witness, Heaven, I have my wish for ever.
Heaven bear witness, so that I may have my wish forever.

JULIA
And I mine.
And so that I may have mine.

Enter Outlaws, with DUKE and THURIO

Outlaws
A prize, a prize, a prize!
We've got a prize, a prize!

VALENTINE
Forbear, forbear, I say! it is my lord the duke.
Stop, stop it, I say! This is my lord the duke.
Your grace is welcome to a man disgraced,

Your grace is welcomed here by a dishonored man,
Banished Valentine.
The exile Valentine.

DUKE
Sir Valentine!
Sir Valentine!

THURIO
Yonder is Silvia; and Silvia's mine.
Silvia is over there; and Silvia is mine.

VALENTINE
Thurio, give back, or else embrace thy death;
Thurio, back off, or else get ready for your death;
Come not within the measure of my wrath;
Don't come within the reach of my anger;
Do not name Silvia thine; if once again,
Do not call Silvia yours; if you do so again,
Verona shall not hold thee. Here she stands;
Verona will not protect you. There she is;
Take but possession of her with a touch:
If you try to take her from me with a touch:
I dare thee but to breathe upon my love.
I dare you do so much as breathe on my love.

THURIO
Sir Valentine, I care not for her, I;
Sir Valentine, I don't love her.
I hold him but a fool that will endanger
I think a man is a fool if he will endanger
His body for a girl that loves him not:
His life for a girl who doesn't love him:
I claim her not, and therefore she is thine.
I'm not taking her, and so she is yours.

DUKE
The more degenerate and base art thou,
You're all the more dishonorable and unworthy,
To make such means for her as thou hast done
That you've gone through all the efforts for her that you have
And leave her on such slight conditions.
And you now give her up with such weak reasoning.
Now, by the honour of my ancestry,

Now, by the honor of my royal birth,
I do applaud thy spirit, Valentine,
I will praise your character, Valentine,
And think thee worthy of an empress' love:
And consider you worthy of an empress' love:
Know then, I here forget all former griefs,
Be aware that I will now forget all former offenses,
Cancel all grudge, repeal thee home again,
Cancel any grudges, and call you back home again,
Plead a new state in thy unrivall'd merit,
And declare that things have changed now that you've show your peerless worth,
To which I thus subscribe: Sir Valentine,
Which I will acknowledge this way: Sir Valentine,
Thou art a gentleman and well derived;
You are a gentleman and of good birth;
Take thou thy Silvia, for thou hast deserved her.
Take Silvia's hand in marriage, for you deserve her.

VALENTINE
I thank your grace; the gift hath made me happy.
Thank you, your grace; the gift makes me happy.
I now beseech you, for your daughter's sake,
I ask you now, for your daughter's sake,
To grant one boom that I shall ask of you.
To grant my one last favor that I will ask of you.

DUKE
I grant it, for thine own, whate'er it be.
I will grant it, for you, whatever it may be.

VALENTINE
These banish'd men that I have kept withal
These banished men that I have lived with
Are men endued with worthy qualities:
Are men who have great qualities:
Forgive them what they have committed here
Forgive them for the crimes they have committed here
And let them be recall'd from their exile:
And let them come home from their exile:
They are reformed, civil, full of good
They are reformed, civilized, and good enough
And fit for great employment, worthy lord.
And suitable for great employment, worthy lord.

DUKE
Thou hast prevail'd; I pardon them and thee:
You have won; I forgive them and you:
Dispose of them as thou know'st their deserts.
Make arrangements for them according to their value.
Come, let us go: we will include all jars
Come on, let's go: we will settle all disagreements
With triumphs, mirth and rare solemnity.
With celebrations, joy and splendid festivities.

VALENTINE
And, as we walk along, I dare be bold
And, as we walk along, I will be brave enough
With our discourse to make your grace to smile.
In your discussions to make your grace smile.
What think you of this page, my lord?
What do you think of this page, my lord?

DUKE
I think the boy hath grace in him; he blushes.
I think the boy is charming; he blushes.

VALENTINE
I warrant you, my lord, more grace than boy.
I promise you, my lord, he has more charms than a boy.

DUKE
What mean you by that saying?
What do you mean by that?

VALENTINE
Please you, I'll tell you as we pass along,
If you'd like, I'll tell you as we walk along,
That you will wonder what hath fortuned.
So that you will marvel at what has happened.
Come, Proteus; 'tis your penance but to hear
Come, Proteus; your punishment is only to hear
The story of your loves discovered:
The story of how you discovered your love:
That done, our day of marriage shall be yours;
When that's over, we will share our wedding day;
One feast, one house, one mutual happiness.
One fest, one house, one shared happiness.

Exeunt

Printed in Great Britain
by Amazon.co.uk, Ltd.,
Marston Gate.